R T

THE DEFINITIVE GUIDE TO CLUB CRICKET

Dan Whiting

Foreword by Jack Brooks

D1419020

For every copy of this book sold, a donation will go to

CONTENTS

INTRODUCTION

Club cricket is our summer sport. With over 15,000 cricket clubs here in the UK and nearly a million people playing the game at an amateur level – not even counting those hardy souls who prop up their local club bar – that is a huge amount of people involved with the game. *The Definitive Guide to Club Cricket* is an invaluable handbook that will help you through the summer (and even the winter). It takes you (in chronological order through the year) from the onset of indoor nets in January, getting the season underway, meeting some of the characters that every club has and picking our way through some of the intricacies of our beloved sport along the way until it's time to pack away the sight screens for another year.

We clubbies even have our own patron saint: St Francis of a CC.

Whether it is the indoor net, the boozy curry, the after-match pint or the rain card, they are all covered here in this guide that should be the Bible of club cricketers across the land (although we don't have any magic tricks in here such as turning fishes into loaves or feeding the five XIs when they all arrive for tea at exactly the same time and thus turning your clubhouse into a feeding free for all akin to the Serengeti).

Having played club cricket for over 30 years for Southgate Adelaide CC who play at the beautiful Walker Cricket Ground in North London and having captained the first XI for six of those years, hopefully I am qualified to give you the lowdown on club cricket. In addition I am now an ECB ACO qualified umpire and I am also the club chairman. All of the characters that you'll read about in this book are real; some of whom I have played with and some against. It's one of the reasons why I love the game.

From the outset, one thing I have to apologise for is my habit of referring to cricketers as blokes. The women's game is thriving and it is great to see; it's just that 99.99% of people that I have played against are male. I think I have played against three or four women in men's cricket over the years. No sexism is intended by this.

Club cricketers come in all shapes, sizes, religions, creeds and colours and as long as you pay your subs, you get to be part of the fun. I'm absolutely chuffed that Jack Brooks agreed to write the foreword for the book. Jack is not only a cricketer who I admire for his attacking bowling style, he is one of the nicest blokes in the game, too. Jack was leading wicket taker for Yorkshire when they won the County Championship in 2014 and 2015 and he came through the club cricket route himself. He is someone who is a beacon of light for all of us clubbies who dream of getting snapped up in the professional game. His rise from the village green to the verge of the England side has been remarkable, yet he remembers his roots. He is someone who has never lost touch with where he came from; a telephone conversation we had about the foreword in June 2016 came about after he had popped back into his club at Tiddington CC in Oxfordshire. No doubt he is destined for a career in media work once his playing days are over as he is great to listen to. Jack is a top bloke – amusing yet informative – and I owe him a pint or two for the foreword.

Oh, and lastly, a portion of the royalties will be going to a wonderful charity called Melanoma UK. Melanoma UK have spent lots of time educating young cricketers and helping those who have suffered from this dreadful disease. It affects many of us who spend hours in the sunshine enjoying our summer sport and they are an extremely worthy cause. Enjoy the book … like a bargain holiday, it's good value, yet the memories will last longer.

Dan Whiting

July 2016

ACKNOWLEDGEMENTS

Big, big thanks go out to the following people without whom, this book would never have happened:

Anthony Morris (aka 'the youth') who has been a major help with this book; Martyn Chandler; Craig Lyte; Tim Grover; Dave Webbing; John Thorp for his articles; Neil Watts; Andy Ferguson; Andy Britton; Darren Close; Adam Burn; Richard Ellwood; Paul Ellwood; Stuart Sumner; Tom Flint; Pat Moran; Stelios; Flacky; Ivan Ninkovic; Matt Jones; Andy Fitz; Matt Fitz; Dave Wilkinson, Liz Fitzpatrick and all the chaps and ladies at Southgate Adelaide CC; to Michelle Tilling for her wonderful editorial work; to the top man Jack Brooks for writing the excellent foreword; to Alex Narey and *The Cricket Paper* for letting me reproduce some of the articles; to Steve Beeston Photography; Steve Gale and Scott Ruskin at Hertford CC; Liam Kenna for starting this writing journey; Paul Ruffhead and Neil Manvell for helping me on a journey through life; Jeff Searle at Amazon; Pinstripe Pete at Botany Bay; Andrew 'Mouse' Craig at North Mymms; Ty Matthews; Matty Duff and his amazing kids; Tom Stillman out in Melbourne; Anthony King in the good ol' US of A; Brett Irwin for his unluckiest dismissal; to Half Time Dileep Pisharody; Steve Kirby for his wonderful stories; John Cosgrove; Steven O'Donoghue; John Simpson at Middlesex for being a generally good bloke; Gill and Mike Nuttall and Andy Worthington at Melanoma UK for the amazing work that they do for this fine charity; Rebecca, Hannah, Ben and Beth Whiting; Slavo; my mum; George Berry; Andy Nash at Somerset CCC, Mike Rutledge at Newport CC (he knows it); Eye Jay and Paul Mokler for their stories; Brian 'Oz' Cohen at North Middlesex; to all at The Tom Maynard Trust, Marcus Charman and the Cricket Family; Hendo, The Bear, Katie, Aatif and all the crew at Guerilla Cricket, Langwith CC; Scott Peters; all those who follow @themiddlestump on Twitter and to all those too numerous to mention who I've played with and against and have given me the stories that make up this book. This one's for you.

FOREWORD

BY JACK BROOKS, YORKSHIRE CCC

If ever there was a book written that was suitable and apt for me to write the foreword for, then it is *The Definitive Guide to Club Cricket*. So when Dan emailed me with the news about his upcoming third book, I was hugely honoured to be asked to pen a few words. I don't know an awful lot about writing or constructing prose, but I have a fair and extensive knowledge of club cricket.

Records show there are approximately a million people who play club cricket in the UK, but in truth that number could be higher with the odd ringer thrown in. There are also 15,000 cricket clubs dotted around the country, but numbers are dwindling as the years go by, as it seems people either no longer want to commit a Saturday or the whole weekend to a game or two of cricket. Society nowadays is unable or not willing to commit this amount of time – there's a lot more going on in the world to distract them. The Sunday friendly game appears to have died out and unless it's a cup or league game, it's rare to see a cricket game on a Sunday these days.

One big question is are we doing enough at grassroots level to get kids interested in playing and keeping them involved through school? State schools will always battle as they struggle for decent facilities and coaching ... and probably a lack of interest. I went to a state school and played only four games against other schools in seven years as a pupil! And I even helped organise a couple of those games.

With cricket being such a technique and skill-based sport and a large amount of equipment being required for a hard ball match it's quite easy to see why some parents either can't or won't commit to spending money on an expensive new bat or schools won't run a team unless they are a specialist sports school, or have a cricket-loving PE teacher who is willing to commit spare time. A massive big up and thank you to any parent or volunteer coach across the land who commits time and energy to getting kids involved, coaching or ferrying them around to various away fixtures.

Having played village cricket back at home in Oxfordshire for Tiddington in the Cherwell League until the age of 21 (and not actually turning professional with Northamptonshire until after a whirlwind trial at the age of 24), I'm quite happy to admit I'm just a glorified club cricketer who got very lucky. Of course I worked hard, listened to advice and tried to be the best I could even when moving on to Oxford CC and representing my county of birth, Oxfordshire. More recently I moved from Northants to Yorkshire but my roots are very much engrained in Tiddington CC, where my parents still live and my brother and some of my best mates still play.

It was at Tiddington where I learnt the game and there are still plenty of enduring memories. Firstly, watching my old man and elder brother Nathan from the boundary edge as a young kid, I would bring my bat and a ball from home and walk about 200 yards to the club telling my Mum I'd be 'back later' on the way out. There would usually be half a dozen or so local kids of dads playing and we would play imaginary Test matches in the practice net in the corner of the ground, then get into trouble with whoever was on tea duty as we tried to pilfer some cakes and sandwiches before the players had any. It always felt like a safe environment in which to play and run amok with other like-minded youths. I think that was the beauty of a village club side, in that it always felt like a family-friendly atmosphere and everyone looked out for each other.

Tiddington have always been a reasonably successful team for the level they play at and have a healthy youth set-up which continually produces players. Over a dozen qualified voluntary coaches all chip in with various age groups from under-9s through to under-17s throughout the week and on Sunday mornings whilst nursing the previous night's excesses. They have never paid players and any overseas lads who come over are amateurs and – other than being given somewhere to live and work – they pay their own way and always leave with an English cricket summer of memories (and usually a few kilograms heavier).

Tiddington is a vibrant social club at the centre of the village – other than the local village pub which doesn't affect trade – where most of the villagers contribute in some way with particular families having been involved for over sixty years. It's this sort of culture which enables this particular club side to survive and thrive. It's always sad to hear of cricket clubs which can no longer afford to continue, or struggle to raise even one side on a Saturday, let alone two or three. For me, any money spent is best put back into the clubs' facilities or hiring a decent ex-professional or overseas to run the coaching and playing side of things. This keeps it organised, rather than hiring mercenaries who leave when the cash dries up and then the club struggles to stay afloat.

I'm sure most club sides have the second or third team captain who on a Friday night or even Saturday morning are still scrabbling around for players. This was my initial route into adult cricket with the 'Dame Thora Hirds' (the 3rd XI). My Dad asked me if I wanted to fill in and I turned up with all the rest of the team, only to be bundled into the back of captain Ray Manning's transit van (which had been transferred into a people carrier with seats and seatbelts installed along each side of the van and kit in the middle). The famous 'Manning Mobile' was a real life adventure every Saturday.

Whatever the result, I'm sure all club sides head back to their own fortress for a jar or two to either celebrate their victory or wallow in how they came up against a team full of guys who were too good for their level and only played as they had to leave early. Stories of dropped catches, calamitous run-outs and jug avoidance no doubt run wild every Saturday night throughout every club side. At least this was always the case 'back in the day' and in recent times the age-old tradition of having a drink with the oppo or even your own teammates appears to be dying out. It's a sad state of affairs and I suppose a way of modern life now that it's just 'not the done thing' anymore, especially after a long day away from friends or family.

Tiddington Cricket Club has always prided itself as 'Oxfordshire's Premier Nightspot' and I'm sure there are still plenty of other club sides lucky enough to have a similar culture – but it's few and far between these days.

One of the highlights for me of my Saturdays playing cricket was the pub crawl back from the away fixture. Within the team convoy a few of the elder players always knew of a good pub or two en route back home and it was inevitable that one or two tactical stop-offs would take place. This just added to the adventure for me, even thought I was invariably sat in the corner of a pub or a beer garden quietly eating a bag of crisps and necking my soft drink, looking up at these men and listening to them talk about the game and general thoughts about cricket and other themes I probably shouldn't have been made aware of. You certainly grow up quicker playing adult sport as a kid!

As I got older the late-night curry order would go around the club bar and an hour or so later the local delivery man would appear to a cheer, carrying what looked like a feast for a thousand in plastics bags and takeaway boxes. Someone would always invite him to stay for a drink or two, but he would run away as quickly as he could! Wise man.

One of the more important members of the club side is the home umpire. My Dad did it when he finished playing and soon ended up umpiring in Premier League cricket which meant he probably wasn't a dodgy biased umpire!

Saying that, I can remember a fair few umpires who would always keep their team in the game or even probably contribute to a few victories with their suspicious decisions. I can remember one such umpire who had officiated for Tiddington through the 1980s and '90s was once heard to remark on field during play to our own bowlers 'if you don't appeal, then I can't give them!'

Needless to say the next batter to get hit on the pads was soon on his way marching back to the pavilion. A bent umpire was a pretty common occurrence and most teams had one. Some were more brazen cheats than others, no doubt, but (in their minds at least) they were all genuine, good men who just had the best interests of their club at heart.

I'll move on to my dealings with Dan Whiting, the esteemed author of this great book. Dan is as mad as a box of frogs. Simply put, he is a bit different in terms of your usual cricket writer and it's no surprise he has built up a fine reputation – mainly due to his growing social media presence since he first arrived on the scene. He is irreverent without being disrespectful and although sometimes I will see a tweet or article that will make me cringe a little, or one which I disagree with as a current professional, I think he is great for the game. There are few like him, willing to divide opinion or speak their mind with a touch of humour and un-PC remarks. It's quite refreshing in this modern world where people constantly have to watch what they say for fear of causing offence. On top of that, Dan actually has a good knowledge of the great game of cricket and is a very passionate man particularly for his club side, Southgate Adelaide CC, based in North London. To add to that he is also now an ECB-qualified umpire, which means he has graduated from the biased, bent old codger he could have been ... which you can never knock. The only real thing I can find wrong with his life choices are that he is a Middlesex cricket fan and a Barnet football fan. He is never shy of a small dig when Middlesex get the upper hand over

Yorkshire (Yorkshire still won the Championship both years) when we play them, and equally when Oxford United have smashed Barnet a few times in the league I tend to send him a gentle reminder ...

Dan first interviewed me for *The Middle Stump* four or five years ago when I was still at Northants trying to find my way in the game. He asked me questions that I had never been asked before. It was actually quite refreshing and interesting to be interviewed by him, albeit over the phone.

He has since written some fine articles for *The Cricket Paper* and is moving onwards and upwards in the cricket fraternity.

Perhaps the best thing that Dan has done since arriving on the scene – and one that I will applaud him for – is his work highlighting melanoma and the causes of skin cancer. I once did a live show with Dan, as a guest alongside Jonny Bairstow, Steve Kirby and Ryan Sidebottom in front of a lively Yorkshire audience at Headingley. Since doing that show, I do what I can to help to promote melanoma awareness, and although not an official ambassador (unlike my team mate Ryan), it's a cause which as a cricketer spending our job in the sun all year round and all over the world, is close to my heart. Jonny is sponsored by the sun care company Uvistat and if it's not his I'm using in the changing room before I take the field, I always make sure I slap on some form of zinc or sun cream, no matter what the weather. At the very least I hope I'm staving off getting leathery skin later in life.

So cheers to Dan and good luck with this book! I have no doubt it will be a success and it really was an honour and privilege to be asked to be involved. Thanks mate.

Brooksy, the glorified clubbie
July 2016

1
THE INDOOR NET

For many a club cricketer, the first glimpse of the coming season will be in early January. Whilst the professionals will start training in November, for us clubbies Christmas is a time for debauchery. In fact most of the year is – but I digress. It is a chance to catch up with old and new team mates.

In early January we dust off the kit bags that have lain dormant in the loft. Christmas, a season that started in the retail industry when the cricket season finished, has now come and gone. For us cricketers, that can only mean one thing ... yes, you guessed it, the indoor nets.

Indoor nets are a strange thing. Yes, they are a hit, and yes they get the cobwebs out of the system but it's not really cricket, is it? They are generally school gymnasiums that are used for nets and this can lead to its own problems. Our nets in recent years have been at a school in North London which has a blue/red/mauve/indigo/maroon-coloured wall, which, when you haven't picked up a cricket bat since September, means you pick up the 200-over-old ball about as well as Stevie Wonder. Ideally the background would be white, cream or even yellow – ironically most probably the same colour as Mr Wonder's bathroom floor.

The feeling of net-related claustrophobia and having your arse repeatedly smacked by the ball from bloke in the next-door net's cut shot (owing to the looseness of the netting) is something that perverts would pay good money for. It's a wonder more sexual deviants haven't been converted to cricket really ... it'd be great value for them at a fiver a week!

Talking of loose nets, the other charming aspect of them is the loose ball when you're batting. If I had a quid for every time one of our quicks has come steaming in, and in mid-stride a ball goes under the netting from the next net and sits there on a length, I would be a rich man. Quick bowlers, not being the brightest of chaps, don't tend to pull out of their delivery, leaving you as confused as all of us are at how Steve Smith scores so many runs for Australia, as you ponder which ball to hit. If you are really unlucky he will hit the said stray cherry, leading to downright, unadulterated chaos.

Then you have the bowlers. Every club in the country will have some bloke who bowls off around 18 yards in the nets. Throw in the fact that they bang it in on a plastic-coated surface and skids through alarmingly, it is often not much fun. Then the said bowler can't work out why, come April, he seems to be suffering a no-ball problem, or bowling half-trackers on a damp one with the ball sitting up and screaming to be pulled, like a night out for those erudite individuals who populate our television screens on such deep-thinking shows such as *Geordie Shore* or *TOWIE*. Likewise, the batsmen who play flowing cover drives on such surfaces that come on beautifully wonder why they keep getting caught in the covers come April, on surfaces that tend to stop.

The other one to watch is the bloke who doesn't bowl much in games but can be quite sharp. This guy will slip you a quick beamer, and having not picked up a bat for four months, you need one of these 'Like a hole in the head', as JFK might have said.
Then you have the two blokes who are there for a chat. The cricket is a sideshow as they stand at the back of the net catching up. Not having seen each other for four months, they discuss everything from football to films to the wife's underwear. If either of these two are allocated to your net then as a batsman you'll get something akin to West Indies' over rate in the early 1980s. Michael Holding off his long run would get through more. Your 15-minute net time will result in a grand total of ten or eleven deliveries from these two.

Due to the timing of the indoor nets, football tends to dominate the conversation. Club rivalry can manifest itself in strange ways and where I live, it is not unknown for Arsenal-supporting quick bowlers to slip Tottenham Hotspur-supporting batsmen a beamer. And vice versa. I can only imagine what must go on in Glasgow.

Then you have the spinners. This man, the king in August and September on turning wickets, spends his indoor net time tugging at the netting like a Grimsby trawlerman as he gets slogged onto the roof of the net by the youngster batting without a care in the world because he will get his 15 minutes of batting time, no matter how many times he is dismissed. In fact, most clubbies prefer to wallop the ball straight away as opposed to practising their forward defensive or the leave outside the off stump.

Lastly, every club across the country will have a few hardy souls who put away the nets, and they're generally the same people who put them out in the first place. Others will clear off every week one minute after the net session is over and they're the same people who become the treasurer's nightmare as he has to chase them for their fiver.

So, as you prepare for the season, remember the above. I am sure this rings true for every cricketer who has ever attended an indoor net session.

2
THE CLUB CAPTAIN

Providing that you have a decent indoor net and don't hit the side netting too often, the first person who you will be in regular contact with is your club captain. The club captain is often a beleaguered man, his wife willing him to resign. In fact, he probably has resigned the job at the end of every season but no one else in the club wants to do it. Despite this, it won't stop critical appraisals of his every wrong move.

There are numerous ways to get in this man's good books. Firstly: have a car. A club captain has to coordinate his bowling changes, his field positions, be a mother, a social worker, a confidant, an organiser, a tactician and a politician, besides finally having to sort out the meet for away games. Organising transport for adults is not in his job specification. Or so he thinks…

The second way is to have a relative of some sort who can make a cricket tea. Stuffing the faces of twenty-six (including umpires and scorers) is never an easy matter and anyone who can do this will make his life easier.

Offering to collect subs and match fees is another way to get into his good books, as is having a good-looking girlfriend who likes to sunbathe on the boundary.

This man is often stressed. Woe betide his sorry little arse if he puts a fielder in the wrong position or inserts the opposition on a hot summer's day and they rack up 280. And as for phoning a result in late to the league, meaning your club gets docked points … well that's high treason. This man wears the pressure of having an entire club resting on his shoulders and it is written all over his face.

No one knows about all the phone calls that he makes to get a side out. He's like a Vietnam veteran on the wire every time his phone bleeps on a Saturday morning. Every call is a potential dropout. This man actually welcomes it when the voice at the other end of the line is talking about mis-sold PPI or some dubious firm of solicitors asking if he has been in an accident recently. This is when he heaves a sigh of relief.

No one sees him visit the ground at 7.30am to check on the state of the pitch after a deluge the previous night. No one sees him having to sit through boring league meetings. This is the man closely clutching a scorebook to his chest throughout the summer months.

There are some perks, however. He can take the credit when the team wins. A slight adjustment to the field resulting in a wicket can make this man look like a tactical genius. He can also choose his position in the batting order. Dropping down the order he at first appears selfless, until you find out that the opposition have a West Indian overseas quick bowler. The really clever ones can adjust this so that they don't have to do an umpiring stint until the end of June, with number four being their position of choice. This means that he can pad up in the hope that his openers bat for twenty overs or so, leaving him to finish off the innings. Even when he does umpire he will only be out there for a four- or five-over stint.

This man is often an isolated individual. Losing friends through dropping them or having rows with them during a cricket season is not unknown and he cuts a sorry, dejected figure when the side loses.

Do not – under any circumstances – phone this man up on a Friday night even if the rain has been of biblical proportions. The reply of 'The game is still on. Yes, of course I know it's raining,'" will be heard regularly by his wife as he slams the phone down for the umpteenth time. Do not turn up late for a meet when the club you are playing is surrounded by roadworks and do not forget your match fees. To see the look on his face when he realises you have one car to transport kit and eleven players to an away match is priceless...

He will often get your name wrong. It is not the only thing that he will forget all season. Match balls and heavy bails are his staple diet. He will often be angry because no one put the covers on the night before, forcing him to bat on a wet one, and he despises the football season, weddings, anniversaries and stag dos. However, when he mentions the words 'club dinner' he will have twenty-five names ready and willing to scoff food.

This man will be your introduction to club cricket.

3
OTHER SKIPPERS

Further down the food chain of cricket clubs you have even more poor, stressed souls than the gentleman mentioned above. Paul Daniels, Paul McKenna and even Paul Collingwood haven't got the magic tricks up their sleeves that the second and third team skippers have as they conjure two sides from seventeen selectable players.

Let's start with the man who runs the 2nd XI. Or the Scooby Doos as they will be known in most clubs – rhyming slang for the 2s. He is often the bridge between the third team and the first team. Requiring Henry Kissinger-style diplomacy skills, he knows that the fracture between the upper echelons of the club and the third team is not unlike that between North and South Korea. He is in the minefield in between and often gets caught up in explosions. He is the glue holding the club together and has to be U Thant, Ban ki-Moon and Kofi Annan all rolled into one as he underpins the club's XIs like some kind of special envoy from the United Nations.

This chap's job is difficult enough, let alone that first-teamer's wedding that can result in the decimation of his team. That's bad enough, but then, despite his players having performed well the previous week, he finds he has to drop people back to the third team the following Saturday, as all the superstars return to 1st-XI action. Alternatively, he can keep them and chuck the odd 1st-XI superstar into the 3rds. Generally this is not a good move and will test his diplomacy skills. Taking the above course of action renders him about as popular as a ginger stepson. Flexibility is his middle name as he is torn between getting results and being a feeder team for the 1st XI. Skippering the Scoobys is one of the toughest jobs in cricket.

Then you have the 3rd XI... Or, depending on the size of your club, skippers who captain the lowest playing XI in the club's structure. Given the choice between this job and being the poor chap who has to clean the toilets after a day's cricket in Kolkata, most sane individuals would choose Eden Gardens and a bogbrush every time.

This guy needs to be a shrewd, skilled operator. He needs contacts and like a good card player, he won't reveal his full hand at selection for fear of losing half of his side later in the week when the higher XIs start suffering from dropouts. He can pull rabbits out of hats just as easily as he can find a player on a Saturday morning and has a treasure trove of cricketing contacts hidden away in his mobile phone. Names from deep within the club's history suddenly turn out for his side.

He finds himself at the mercy of higher XIs and often goes out with a team of kids. This man needs to drive. It is a prerequisite of the role when you have a lot of youngsters. He can find his side can win games easily by ten wickets or lose by a similar score. The results have nothing to do with the skill of his cricket side but he is at the mercy of GCSEs, A-levels and the like.

Every cricket club has their own version of this person. He is a stressed individual and can often do a passable impression of Lord Lucan on a Saturday morning so the other skippers don't have the opportunity to steal his players. In the law of the cricketing captain jungle, he is at the bottom of the food chain. He's the vulture who has to pick the bones of the rest of the club after the lions and the hyenas have had the best bits off the carcass. Despite the public offerings of a united club, he is fully aware that there are three individual teams out there and the smooth flow of players moving seamlessly between teams is not for him.

However, for all his faults, this man is a bloody legend. Every club needs this guy and every cricketer started off in his XI. He is part of the furniture and cricket as a sport, is richer for having these individuals with them.

4
THE FIRST WEEKEND OF SUMMER

For the club cricketer the cricket season can start either with a friendly in April or for some they are straight into a league match, not turning out until early May. Some may even be later, especially those for whom football takes precedence over cricket. However, whenever you start I can guarantee that you will fall into one of two camps. Just in the way that you can't be a little bit pregnant – you are or you're not – cricketers on the first game of the season are judged in the same manner. Yes, it comes down to those who have netted and those who haven't.

Those who have netted have already made fools out themselves in the more private setting of a school gymnasium back in January among their teammates. Not for them is the public show of idiocy. For these people the indoor net is a completely different kettle of fish from playing outdoors. As mentioned in the opening chapter, it is one of the few environments where you see the 4th XI's nine, ten or jack trying to grind it out against the 1st XI opening bowler, often in poor lighting against that 200-over-old ball and coming out of a multi-coloured background. Every club has a bowler who regularly hits the side netting. Every club has a net bowler who is quite sharp and slips you a beamer. Every club has a quickie who bangs it in on plastic-coated surfaces and wonders why he keeps getting pulled for fours or sixes come April when the ball stops on a slow pitch.

Then you have the other camp – those who haven't given a thought to the summer game until the night before. Whilst the professionals might swan off to Dubai and South Africa on pre-season tours to get some outdoor warm-up matches under their belts, warm weather training for these individuals normally entails a pint in front of a pub's open fire.

Every club has them and every club also has the following individuals:

The first one is the bloke who forgot to wash his kit at the end of last season. Just about avoiding injuries going into the loft and retrieving his kit from under the Christmas tree, he pulls out his kit on the morning of the opening weekend to find that last season's wet towel combined with cricket whites have cultivated some sort of fungi that has spread not only to his kit but to his whole loft causing rising damp in neighbouring houses. A last-minute dash to the sports shop is his warm-up and normally he arrives to the opening game £300 lighter.

The second individual is the man who tears in off 25 yards. It is not the only thing he tears as you will no doubt hear the ping of his hamstring keeping him out until mid-July at the earliest.

The third is the man who has forgotten his technique and leaves not so much a gate as a portcullis, requiring him not to trouble the scorers on his first outing. It is only then he regrets not turning up for that winter net.

You also have the youngster who turns up to cricket in shorts, sunglasses and a T-shirt (because that's what he did last season) only to find that the April average nightly temperature of 4°C leaves him a tad chilly as he leaves the clubhouse at 10.30pm at night.

Finally, you have the player who turns up in a short-sleeved shirt and enjoys his fielding experience as much as Mike Gatting enjoys the Rosemary Conley diet. Having played myself in the snow once as a teenager, I now pack at least three T-shirts, two shirts, a short-sleeved and a long-sleeved jumper for the opening encounter. I might look like the Michelin man, but I don't care. Experience has also taught me never to field in the gulley in weather this cold. Wherever you field you are praying that it isn't slapped at you too hard, but only the bravest get their hands to a full-blooded cut in the gulley in April.

At our club in North London we once had an Australian overseas player who debuted in a game played in just 5°C. I asked him if he had ever played cricket in weather so cold and he replied, 'Mate, I've never played rugby in weather that cold.' He started to enjoy the season around the middle of July.

I have even known of people doing the scoring in cars due to weather being so cold. An acknowledgement of the umpire's signal is given by beeping the horn, although the flashing of headlights on dark days has also been known. Perhaps it's surprising that more scorers haven't been converted to 'dogging'...?

The first game of the season can be a culture shock in many ways. Having spent the winter with mature and sophisticated adults, you find yourself regressing into teenage behaviour quite quickly when back amongst the boys. Middle-aged men would never set fire to a workmate's newspaper as they were reading it and no one in their right mind would press a hot teaspoon against their wife's arm having stirred a cup of tea, yet in the cricket changing room this quickly becomes the norm and the source of much mirth. Plenty of stories, true and apocryphal, are regaled as six months' worth of pent-up laughter and frustration is released.

Then you have the cricket. This is the time of year for the trundler, a man in his element on these green-tops. The opening batsman, having patted the ball back to him for five overs, eventually chips one back to mid-off. Alternatively he thinks it is mid-July and in the first over with a booming off drive, he chips one to mid-off. Finally, you get those who stop their shot half way through and you've guessed it – they chip one to mid-off.

Afterwards you have the following days to get through. I have seen many a cricketer walk in to work at the end of April doing a more than passable impression of John Wayne as the skipper has forgotten to include a wicketkeeper, press-ganging some poor individual in to it. The ageing opening bowler finds he can finally walk normally by the following Friday, yet warm-ups and warm-downs are rare in club cricket. Let alone the dreaded ice bath.

Workmates don't understand that intercostal muscles, calves and a variety of other body parts are used during a game of cricket and are short on sympathy for the ageing cricketer. Even an average day on the field at club level requires you to walk 10 or 11 miles. Again this is a culture shock for the man who hasn't netted and his Fitbit shows that he has accumulated a princely sum of 400 steps in his office job.

This will be the average welcome that is given to the clubbie.

5
THE LAST-MINUTE DASH

As mentioned briefly in the previous chapter you'll find numerous clubbies from various opponents within your area in a sports shop on the morning of the opening game of the season. It is the time of year that they realise that their spikes have worn down to roughly 4mm in depth and will leave them like Bambi on ice on a wet April outfield. You bump into lots of old mates from rival clubs and even some of your own team mates, too. This opening day bonanza is the cricketing equivalent of a mad rush in the Christmas sales in most stores.

It's only when the clubbie arrives at the ground for the first match of the season that he discovers the optimism of buying 34in waist trousers doesn't equate with his winter's excesses. He quickly realises how unfit he has actually become, as his waist size creeps nearer to 40in. You might even hear the audible tear of new whites from the slip cordon as the clubbie crouches down in readiness for the first delivery.

Many clubbies' whites are actually ruined in these first few dank games as the wet spring ground muddies that pristine new long-sleeved jumper. It's often at this time of the season that the clubbie forgets that cricket trousers aren't tailor-made, and with no wife or mother in the dressing room to turn up the hem, many a clubbie can be seen with bell-bottomed whites akin to a 1970s glam rock star, with a good 10–12in of excess cloth flapping about round their new boots.

It is not unknown for the clubbie to go arse over tit the first time he tries to chase a ball to the boundary in this instance.

6
THE CHARACTERS OF A CRICKET DRESSING ROOM

As well as the stressed captains mentioned earlier, there's pretty much a stereotype for every one of your team mates. Not only this, but they are mirrored in the opposition. Here they are broken down to what you can expect as a clubbie to be sharing your summer with;

The Opening Bat – a dour, grumpy type, he is often without humour. For him, he has spent many an afternoon out in the first over only to stand at slip as he doesn't bowl. For the privilege he is asked to pay £11, or whatever his match fee is and as such will often bring a book or a newspaper with him. He is grumpy because he spends a lot of his time having to grind out the new ball or to do a job against the best attacks on wet wickets. You can often find him in the dressing rooms peppered with a map of balls ranging from his inner thigh to his ribs. His profession will normally be anything that doesn't involve talking to people.

The Boring Number Three – an accountant by trade, this bloke will show you his forward defensive all day long. He turns up to practice and his 20 minutes of batting will consist of 10 minutes of leaving the ball followed by 10 minutes of forward defensives. A lover a not out, he will often be top of the averages, despite having scored fewer runs than three of his team mates. He knows the value of statistics and is often spotted having a half of real ale after a game before going back to his equally boring wife. She will be seen once a season at the club dinner only to be offended by the raucous behaviour amongst the boys. Generally doesn't play on a Sunday as it interferes with his bell-ringing at church. A school governor and a pillar of the community.

The Middle-Order Dasher – this chap will spend his summer travelling to games in his sports car with the roof pulled down, whatever the weather. Public school-educated, he will have a range of shots with a high elbow from years of having the best coaching that his father could buy him. Generally a smashing chap, he can often disappear at the end of a match as he has a date with a young lady by the name of Jemima or Henrietta. Has been known to bat in a quartered or hooped cap. Will often be regaling the dressing room with his exploits with the aforementioned young ladies the previous night. Works as 'something in the City'.

The Middle-Order Bosher – likes to bat at number six and prefers to score through the leg side. How many times have we all had the opposition at 20-4 and then this bloke walks in and smashes it all around the ground for a quick 70? Often with forearms like Popeye and a 3lb bat, he looks at boundary fielders as something to take on and not there to have a single pushed to. Often a man to be beaten to the tea interval by his team mates as they know there will not be much left after he has filled his considerable boots. In days of old this man would have been the village blacksmith.

The Fat Wicketkeeper – small bloke who was quite a decent keeper when he was young but the years of the pub and the curry house have taken their toll on his body. Still a decent gloveman, he struggles down the leg side due to his considerable weight, although his low centre of gravity helps him with the ball that keeps low, should his gut not get in the way. This man doubles up as the rugby club prop forward or hooker and has a decent line in chat, one-liners and comebacks. He has seen and heard it all before. Again this is a man you want to beat to the table at the tea interval. He is often a builder.

The Gobby Spinner – generally a bit of a loose cannon, this man would love to be able to unleash a bouncer when he gets clattered for a six but has to use his guile and cunning instead. Constantly probing and asking questions, and that's just to the umpire who turns down his lbw appeals all afternoon. Often the joker of the changing room and on the pitch too. Generally at the heart of any rumbles with the opposition due to a sharp word somewhere. Works in sales.

The Gobby Kid – the star of his age group all through club cricket and doesn't he know it? Often playing adult cricket at the age of 15 or 16 he is the best fielder in the side by a long chalk, before the days of booze and curries have got to him. Despite the outer confidence this is a thin veneer and underneath he can crack. Wizened members of the opposition know this and can reel him in like a trout with a fly. They often do. He can also be the butt of jokes from The Gobby Spinner and looks up to the Middle-Order Dasher. He's often a schoolboy who can be spotted filling up the fruit and vegetable aisle of a supermarket on weekday evenings.

The Dour Bowler – hates going for runs. Has often played a higher standard of cricket and still knows what to do with the ball but has lost his pace somewhat. This bloke would rather bowl a maiden than take a wicket. Misfields see him go redder than an alcoholic in the sun and he's constantly grunting and chattering to himself on his way back to his mark. He often has a moustache. Often this man will be a maths teacher.

The Quick Bowler – can often be as thick as shit, he will spend a lot of time with the opening bat despite them being polar opposites in education, class and character. He will never read his paper unless it is a tabloid and will be discussing the merits of today's Page 3 stunner. Generally has a short temper and has been known to miss the odd game for disciplinary reasons. If you drive this bloke for four through the covers on the front foot you know the next ball will be a short one. He likes violence and can often be spotted turning up for a game with a black eye. Unemployed.

7
THE CRICKET TEA

No other game in the world stops for food apart from cricket. If you play Premier League cricket you'll find yourself probably stopping for a bit of lunch as well. If your team mates look like they have overcome a bout of anorexia nervosa, then the chances are that your club puts on a decent spread.

At professional level the lunches tend to be healthy these days. Chicken, fish and pasta are the norm and long gone are the days of Nancy's famous Lord's lunches where Gatt would have a couple of roast dinners followed up by a couple of bowls of spotted dick and custard. At club level, though, things are different.

A club cricket tea is index linked. In my league you can't charge more than £40 to the opposition so with your £40 too, you have to use your imagination to feed twenty-six ravenous cricket-related gannets. Clubs are having to think about it and they are doing so very well. The standards of club cricket teas have improved considerably over the years.

Back in the 1980s, the standard fare was sandwiches. Often you'd ask someone if it was a decent tea and the response of, 'Yes, relentless sarnies,' would come forth. This might be topped up with a scone and a bit of jam or back in those days a Jacob's Club biscuit or a Wagon Wheel, and I'm not talking about the graph that good scorers show where you have hit the ball. There wasn't much in the way of cultural awareness and a plate of ham sandwiches didn't go down too well if you were playing a side consisting of eleven Muslims.

Curled-up sandwiches were run of the mill, or if clubs were feeling particularly flash they'd experiment with a ploughman's. Most of the time it was some limp, decaying salad that came with a free hair from the tea lady. And that's if you were lucky.

Now, however, there is plenty of variation and scope for all who play the game and it is great to see. Chicken wings, samosas, onion bhajis, pakoras and a wealth of other goodies have entered into the summer game grub. Chicken nuggets have also come into play but with the cost of a cricket tea involved, these no doubt come from a low-cost supermarket. Despite the fact that cricketers are probably eating claws, beaks and that red bit from on top of the chicken's head, a plate of these goes down quicker than an Italian centre-forward in the penalty box. Fresh fruit is fairly common, as is a decent salad.

Some clubs try to keep it healthy with a pasta option but at many there is a selection of chocolate cake, coffee cake and walnut cake to try to weigh down the opposition opening bowler for his post-interval spell. One club I know of, involved in an important promotion-chasing game, even undercooked the sausages in a bid to try to scupper the opposition. It's advisable to trust only teas that are on one plate for both sides to select from.

With just a 20-minute interval in league cricket, tea is similar to watching a Labrador devour his daily bowl.

The type of tea that you get often depends upon the opposition. At my club in Southgate in North London, the ground is located in an area which is heavily populated by Greek Cypriots. Quite regularly now we have a tea offering a Greek salad and the sight of feta cheese scattered around the carpet of our clubhouse is a common occurrence. Playing against an Indian side offers some fantastic new delicacies to your average clubbie. A West Indian side will offer plenty of chicken and rice, while if the opposition have a couple of fat lads in the side you can bet your bottom dollar that there are some cream cakes on offer.

Unusual and new elements being added into a cricket tea can often cause confusion and chaos amongst certain members of your team. At one away ground one of our members piled his plate up with spicy potato wedges. With cream put out next to the jam for the scones, unfortunately this chap thought it was mayonnaise to accompany the wedges and put large dollops of it all over his carb-loaded tea. It wasn't the best move.

A cricket tea can work its way through the digestion system fairly quickly after the interval. Many a club opening batsman has pulled out of a delivery due to an audible fart emanating from the slip cordon, while it has been known for bowlers to run off the pitch hurriedly looking for a change of whites, desperately clutching around the back of his trousers so his team mates don't see the collateral damage caused by his latest indiscretion.

The cricket tea is here to stay and despite being much maligned, it is the staple diet of clubbies all across the world. For many of us, it will be the only thing that you eat on a Saturday until that team bonding curry at 11pm. A couple of sandwiches isn't going to soak up the amount of beer that most clubbies indulge in on a Saturday night, therefore it is imperative that you line your stomach. Just as good batsmen play themselves in, good captains bat themselves lower down the order at places where they know they are going to get a good tea. Good drinkers offer themselves up as good team men by advising the skipper that it is time to let the youngsters have a go and line their gut in advance of their night's alcohol consumption.

Like Wimbledon, a holiday with the kids or a barbecue, the cricket tea is part of your summer.

8
THE RAIN CARD

Early in the cricket season inclement weather can play a huge part in the life of a clubbie. Your weekend will often be made or ruined by the vagaries of the weather. It can be the difference between the glory of a century or having to take the kids to a cinema to watch yet another Pixar film.

On a Friday night as rain, hail and even snow lashes the cricket pitches of our green and pleasant land, numerous club cricketers will be holed-up in public houses, bars and at home having a couple of pre-match drinks. For some, the quiet Friday night turns into a more boisterous affair and as one or two 'liveners' turn into seven or eight, the hopes and prayers will turn from wishing for a run about on a Saturday afternoon, to selling your soul to the devil in the hope that the game is called off. For those of us in the know, this is called playing the rain card.

The rain card is the gamble of boozing heavily on a Friday night in the hope that your Saturday is washed out by rain. It is a card played throughout club cricket and has been since time immemorial. No doubt it will be played for a number of years in the future, too.

It is not just those of us of an amateur level who wish to gamble with their averages. At Centurion Park in South Africa a few years ago, South Africa played England in a game that became infamous for being fixed by Hansie Cronje. After South Africa batted on the first day, heavy rain – well known to those who have visited this continent – poured down for three days. With the ground under water and thinking that it would be a washout, a number of the visiting England players took themselves off to various watering holes in the Pretoria region and proceeded to get, in what's known as layman's terms, shedded.

One of the aforementioned players was Darren Gough, who had been out drinking with Ian Woosnam. 'Woosie' wasn't just the nickname that the golfer went by as Gough had to play through a torrid time. Without knowing that the opposition captain was desperate for a result, as he admitted afterwards for a few rand and a leather jacket, Gough woke up in horror as the rain clouds had disappeared and the submerged ground was drying out rapidly. With a hangover thumping his head under a hot African sun, the bowler just about made it onto the field of play having ejected the contents of his stomach of the previous night's excesses and was made to bowl by a furious Nasser Hussain.

Luckily for the Barnsley quick, Cronje did a deal where he declared and after negotiations to forfeit the innings, Gough actually ended up hitting the winning runs.

He wasn't the only one.

Phil Tufnell was well known for a fist pumping action and the cry of 'Yessss' as he watched the weather forecast with rain predicted for the following day. Tufnell's nights out were regularly planned – in their magnitude and timing – around the meteorological forecasts. He was a regular purveyor of the rain card. Tuffers would go and drink like a fish if dictated to by Michael Fish, so one Middlesex regular would often remark.

Andrew Flintoff, when skippering England in Australia, was allegedly another who played the rain card, whilst Ian Botham just played the card, no matter the weather; taking the best player from the opposition with him apparently, with the express intention of getting him in no state to be at his professional best the following day.

Others from the Botham era haven't been so lucky with their gambles though. A John Player League game at Cheltenham College in the mid-1980s between Gloucestershire and Leicestershire has been talked about in cricketing circles for years. A lunchtime downpour of biblical proportions sent the players of both sides scuttling for the sponsors' tents and with the ground under water they took full advantage of the hospitality. The likes of David Gower got a liking for the fine wines on offer, yet to his chagrin the umpires came in a couple of hours later and announced that they would be having a ten-over thrash in an hour or so if no more rain came down.

Having changed into whites and tried to sober, sorry warm up, one Gloucestershire fielder was a casualty as a high catch hit him straight between the eyes. The watching Andy Stovold, who was there with his family on a Sunday afternoon jaunt, was press-ganged into action. Allegedly he was the only sober player on the ground.

When the game finally started, Gower allegedly tried to sweep the first ball and promptly fell over to much hilarity from all of those in the know. Apparently it wasn't his most graceful innings. The result of the game can't even be remembered by those who played, but this game is infamous in rain card circles.

For the club cricketer, he often doesn't know if his rain card was worth playing. Cunning cricket committees up and down the country often won't call a game off until the last minute, hoping that the boys will stay in the bar. Despite games being totally unplayable by 5pm on a Friday afternoon, there have been some clubs who still insist on their players arriving at the ground at midday on the Saturday. They do this knowing full well that the less disciplined members of the side will part with their hard-earned cash over the club bar. Naturally this is all done in the art of 'team bonding' and good club men will start proceedings by plonking a jug on the table. This brings other gambles into play and at least one that has resulted in divorce. I'm talking about lying to one's partner over your whereabouts on a Saturday afternoon.

Many a club cricketer will have been picked up by their partner on a Saturday evening having spent the previous six or seven hours with his team mates in the club bar. This is despite the fact that his wife or girlfriend thinks he has been playing cricket. 'We ummed and ahhed, had a look and then it rained even more,' mumbled through the fumes of seven pints has been quoted to many a young lady by the club player in a desperate attempt to get out of being dragged around a retail park while his game has been washed out.

The more cunning clubbie will wash his whites in a puddle by the club bar to try to outfox his partner, whilst at one Hertfordshire cricket club the well-known trick of going to get the boundary rope in while still dressed in whites is a convincing enough way of getting them dirty and giving the impression that you've actually played.

Certain clubs I know have a policy that no reports of games being abandoned should be put on social media. This comes from both the club itself and the players. Youngsters are admonished and warned that in no circumstances should this be mentioned on Facebook, Twitter or other avenues to the outside world and by doing so, you'd be letting your team mates down.

For the experienced rain card player, there is nothing worse than Friday night rain with sunshine forecast for a Saturday morning. This is a lottery. This is the equivalent of an opening batsman grinding it out on a difficult wicket or a bowler having to bowl line and length on a road. Only the very best get this right.

So the rain card is a difficult one to judge. It is an art and has various derivations as we have seen. As the saying goes. 'If you dance with the devil, you will get burned.'

I am sure there are plenty of club players who will feel the heat over the summer months.

9
THE UNFUNNIEST PEOPLE IN THE WORLD

Sooner or later playing club cricket you will play at a ground with a road. At least once a season (if you're lucky) a car will drive past and one of the occupants will yell out of the window, 'Owzat?'. These are the unfunniest people in the world. That is all that needs to be said on the matter.

10
THE OVERSEAS PLAYER

At some point if you play club cricket you're going to come into contact with an overseas player. They play for your club or may be in the opposition ranks, but you will have some sort of integration with people from different parts of the world. Not being one to generalise in any shape or form, here is the lowdown to what you can expect from your new international friend.

The Australian – as a teenager brought up on the relaxed, surf-loving, beach bum, *Home and Away* or *Neighbours* type of Aussies we came to know and love in the 1980s, it can often be a culture shock when this mild-mannered, polite chap crosses the boundary. One thing about Aussies is that they all suffer from white line fever. They are competitive, hard and above all, great to play cricket with. Although saying that, some of their rhetoric can leave a bit to be desired. No Shakespearean soliloquies will come from this gentleman, and neither does he offer the wit of Oscar Wilde – rather he prefers to call you various vulgarisms for the female genitalia in the first over before questioning everything from your parentage to your sexual technique/orientation. Aussies like a beer after the game and this rabid lunatic on the pitch suddenly transforms back into a polite individual. Many Aussies are fond of the phrase, 'Shithouse'. This can either be used as a noun or an adjective. It can be a place to visit after a few eskis or the prawns not being done well enough on a Barbie, or it can be his appraisal of your batting technique after he beats you outside the off stump.

The New Zealander – the Kiwi is very different from an Australian. They are far more relaxed, although mistakenly call a Kiwi an Aussie and you will soon feel their wrath. Not many Kiwis get worked up about stuff, apart from calling them Aussies. Oh, and rugby. If you share a season with a New Zealander when the British Lions are touring over there, it can be a grim experience for us Brits. The Kiwi cricketer also likes a beer as well as some interesting types of cigarette. When out for a low score, he might even disappear around the back of the pavilion as plumes of marijuana smoke fill the car park. Not known for buying his round at the bar. Often these people will be on a UK passport, meaning they don't have to play as an overseas player. Many of the Kiwis from the South Island have Scottish ancestry, such as Brendon McCullum. Only the Scots, at a time when Britain ruled the world and could have chosen anywhere on the whole planet, would think, 'I know – let's go somewhere even colder than Scotland'. Dunedin and Invercargill right at the bottom of the South Island aren't the places to take your shorts and flip flops.

The West Indian – these guys can light up a cricket dressing room. Get two or three of them together at cricket and you will hear laughter all day. They can be most amusing and will often introduce various West Indian food to the team. Don't be surprised when that spotty, pubescent youth in your side who has lived on a pre-match diet of McDonald's for years suddenly starts dining on fried plantain, salt fish and ackee and the odd yam, having spent a month or so with his new-found mate from the Caribbean. The West Indian will have the odd cold one after the game or maybe even a rum, but the foremost thing he will have on his mind is introducing himself to the local female population. Like Wayne Daniel at Middlesex in the 1970s and '80s, these men are loved by their team mates, if not the husbands of the many English lady friends that they acquire during their stint in the UK. Your local glazier will love having a West Indian in town if your ground borders neighbouring houses, often paying for his air fare himself. West Indian lads love to belt the ball and if you are an umpire of a side with one of these guys in the team, expect to be raising both of your arms above your head on a regular basis over a summer.

The Pakistani – often excitable, these guys also play cricket in a West Indian fashion. Pakistani cricketers will bring along a bat the size of a railway sleeper and swish it around like Zorro. When they connect they are liable to bring down light aircraft they hit it so far. Every club cricketer will be familiar with the words 'Shabash' meaning well done or bravo, or even come on. For many of us it is the only Urdu word that we know, although anyone who has spent time watching Wasim and Waqar hoop the ball around corners a few years ago will also know 'Pakistan Zindabad', which translates as

'Long live Pakistan!' Pakistanis are interesting cricketers. They light up the cricket pitch, but don't expect to see them in the bar after a match. It's a genuine wonder how these guys run around a pitch for six or seven hours during the fasting month of Ramadan and then not even have a drink of water. Respect these guys and you will get a hell of a lot back.

The Indian – the Indian is hard to pin down as it is such a diverse country. The advent of IPL has caused these guys to start to smash the ball to all corners. There is no Sunil Gavaskar-style blocking now as the Indian opener did in the 1975 World Cup and ended up on 36 not out after 60 overs. The Indian will have a post-match beer and can often bring some interesting food into a cricket club, too. He is a competitor and loves winning. The Indian cricketer will be a polite, quiet, charming individual when his family is around and as soon as they are out of sight will have a beer and a fag. He has been known to introduce cricket equipment into the dressing room, buying it at home before selling it on to his UK team mates at a profit. Bats as thick as a viking's oar suddenly become the norm. One Indian who came over here was the well-heeled and high-caste Sourav Ganguly. When he arrived at Lancashire, he asked Mike Atherton to carry his kit from the car to the dressing room despite Athers having amassed numerous Test caps at this point. He was promptly told to "Fuck off". Get an Indian over from the south of the country and you will be introduced to some of the finest grub known to mankind. These guys are obsessed with cricket.

The South African – satirical puppet show *Spitting Image* may have told us in the 1980s that 'I've never met a nice South African', but on the club circuit you will meet plenty. These guys are as strong as an ox and like to eat meat. Finding them putting their hand up to buy a round of drinks at the bar can be as rare as a lion likes his zebra steak, but they are good guys to have on your side. The Saffa can also be a fearsome sledger with a ball in his hand with many an English clubbie finding himself on the wrong end of a stream of Afrikaans invective, interspersed with the phrase 'doos'. The South African overseas player often tells it how it is. As English we are modest about our cricketing exploits, so imagine my surprise once when asking an opposition Saffa if he had got many runs whilst over here. Modesty wasn't for him – we were all expecting 'Well, a few here or there,' but he responded with 'Fucking loads.' With wickets in South Africa bouncing a lot more than those over here, expect your South African to get bowled a lot when he first arrives in the UK, going on the back foot to balls that pitch just short of a length. Some work it out quickly and some don't. You never know what you are going to get with a Saffa. As one chap from a neighbouring club told me, 'sometimes they are Shaun Pollock, and sometimes they are a load of bollocks.'

The Sri Lankan – introducing a food to your cricket club similar to that of South India, I love Sri Lankans and their attitude to the game. Generally very popular in the dressing room, they like a laugh too. Muttiah Muralitharan at Lancashire became part of the culture there and was good mates with Andrew Flintoff. As he came out to bat at number eleven in a Test match in Galle, Freddie asked him how he was going to bat today: 'Today I am slogging' was the response from Murali. With wristy batsmen, mystery spinners and decent seamers, this small island punches above the weight of Rangana Herath and Aravinda de Silva combined, when it comes to producing decent cricketers. Get a Sri Lankan over to your club and you will be a richer man for the experience. Befriend him and go and visit him in his country. It is a beautiful island and a Test match at Galle is a must for everyone who loves their cricket.

11
ONE BRINGS TWO

Fielding sides often go quiet when you have been chasing leather for hours in 30°C. In an attempt to rally the troops, when the opposition are 180-1 you will hear the cry 'Come on lads, one brings two' as the skipper urges his bowler to take a wicket. It has rarely been proved right.

12
THE AWAY GAME

A trip to another club might happen early in your club career, or it could even be your first match. It normally involves a flustered captain trying to marshal the troops as eleven bedraggled souls enter the car park one by one. That is, if the skipper is lucky. The meet time for an away game is often under or over done by a good hour. Sometimes a 5-mile trip will involve a meet at 11.30am for a 1.30pm start, whereas I have known of clubs travelling the distance of the county and meeting at 12.00pm. In my experience, this ends badly. Every club in the world has the following within their ranks:

Mark Thatcher – named after the ex-Prime Minister's son who famously got lost in the Sahara Desert, most sides have an individual who always pretends that he knows where he's going. In reality he doesn't have a clue. Never, ever let this man lead the convoy as he will reduce your warm-up and stretching time. He has been responsible for many an opening bowler's torn hamstring.

Mark Thatcher Mark Two – this guy will get the name of the venue that you're due to visit wrong, taking you completely to the wrong place. Three gentlemen at our club went to a ground at Batchworth once instead of Datchworth, a mere 25 miles away. Ex-England cricketer Chris Lewis once ended up in Newport in South Wales instead of Newport in Shropshire where an England training camp was taking place. This was no fewer than 150 miles in the wrong direction.

Ayrton Senna – his last words on leaving the clubhouse will be, 'I know where it is lads, just follow me.' It's at this point that, instead of leading the convoy, he jumps the lights outside your club and tears off into the distance at great speed, leaving three or four cars behind him stuck at a red light, without a clue where they are going.

The Rip van Winkle – 15 minutes after the meet time this man is woken by a telephone call from his screeching skipper demanding to know where he is. Often this'll be a man who doesn't drive or is so hungover that he couldn't possibly get into his car. Faced with the option of going with ten men, the skipper has no choice but to wait for him at the club, meaning that the whole team turn up late for the game.

The Fat Bastard – despite you running horrendously late for your away game, this bloke knows he isn't going to get fed until tea. He therefore punctuates his journey with a visit to the drive-through of a well-known fast-food chain. This again causes lateness, which means further stress and anxiety for your skipper.

The People Carrier – many a clubbie in lower XIs is picked due to the fact that he has a big car. No matter what his form is like, the fact that he has a seven-seat people carrier and can get kit into his automobile means his place in the side is safe.

The Snail – despite running late due to a Rip van Winkle, this man has no concept of urgency. The scenic route or taking a highway full of roadworks is his usual method of travel and will still drive at 28mph despite the skipper urging him to put his pedal to the metal.

The Tearaway – often a youngster who has just passed his driving test, this man is the antithesis of the Snail. Terrifying his passengers, the last thing they want to do is play cricket after a journey with this chap. One of my ex-team mates once threatened to fight 'a tearaway' after he clocked 140mph on the A1 on the way back from a game.

The Clueless Skipper – this is a man without any concept of a major event taking place en route to your game. A game in West London will always involve a quick look to see if any football match is taking place at Wembley, or, for a visit to a Hertfordshire ground, you'll need to see if a concert is taking place at Knebworth House. Needless to say, this guy's blood pressure went through the roof as eleven of us tried to navigate our way through 100,000 people going to an Oasis gig back in the 1990s.

The Alzheimer's Skipper – as a 12-year-old, I was a scorer for a club in North London. Imagine my sheer panic when I suddenly looked around the opposition clubhouse and found out that my team had all left without me. My mother, who was due to pick me up from the home clubhouse, was none-too-impressed either when all of the cars returned back there *sans* me. A phone call was made from the club in question to our club and things were sorted out. Luckily, the chairman of the club offered to pay for a taxi, which he kindly did, but not before the skipper received a major bollocking for leaving a kid behind.

The introduction of satnav systems have helped the club cricketer vastly in this regard, but they can't eradicate lateness. Do yourself and your skipper a favour and arrive 5 minutes earlier than the meet time. Your place in the batting order might depend on it.

13
OUT THREE TIMES IN ONE BALL

Recently our club played a game where a member of the opposition was 'out' three times and had only faced one ball. Coming in to bat he found himself at the non-striker's end. On the last ball of the over his partner called him through for a quick single and despite him being a yard out of his ground, he was given not out by their umpire. The first ball of the next over his partner drove a straight drive back which flicked the bowler's finger and went on to the stumps. Despite the bowler's near-dislocated finger, again their umpire denied that he had got a touch on it and gave him not out. Eventually he got down to the striker's end and was cleaned up on his first ball, to much merriment from the fielding side. Justice eventually prevailed.

14
KIT

Some cricket club changing rooms look like a sale in a charity shop – which, ironically, is where you will be able to pick this book up in a few years' time priced at 30p. A charity shop that is, not a cricket changing room. Cricket changing rooms can be messy places at times with clothes strewn everywhere, wet towels lying on floors, discarded shower gels stolen from hotel rooms on tour and empty cans of deodorant.

A lot of cricketers have one thing in common – an all-consuming obsession with kit. You will find many jokes and japes amongst players, but kit is reasonably sacrosanct and joking around with other people's equipment is deemed out of order. Saying that, I have had shower gel in my batting gloves before and Deep Heat in my helmet, which after 10 minutes' worth of sweating made my eyes a tad sore. Generally though, kit is not to be messed with.

Bats can be fiddled with, messed around with, tinkered with and ruined. An extra grip here, shaving a bit off the bottom there, sanded down, over oiled, not to mention those woodpeckers of players who spend their days knocking in a new bat with a mallet and ruining the peace for all and sundry. There will always be one player in every team that people take their stuff to. This chap will have scissors, spike tighteners, razor blades, cones and a host of other implements. Not only that, he'll also be able to roll a grip on to a bat handle quicker than he can roll his own foreskin back. One search of this man's kit by the boys in blue and he would be looking at a long prison sentence for the selection of offensive weapons in his kit bag.

Bats now come in all shapes and sizes and there are far more options available with the advent of hand-made bats from small, independent bat makers. The days of Stuart Surridge Jumbos crashing the ball around have long gone. About 30 years ago the only bats you ever saw at club level were Gray-Nicolls, Gunn & Moore, the garishly coloured orange and black Newbery, County, Slazenger and a plethora of Duncan Fearnley Magnums. Adidas were sticking to tennis gear, although some clubbies would use a pair of their Stan Smith trainers occasionally. The more cunning ones would even rip the Velcro fastener as the ball beat the bat in a bid to try and con the umpire that the striker had nicked off to the keeper.

I have always preferred Gunn & Moore as my stick of choice after a Slazenger V12 I had only struck the ball about as far as cover (if you really timed it). I'm not saying it was a bad bat, but it was the best one that I have ever had for playing the spinners with a host of catchers around the bat, as the ball would regularly just plop down at my feet.

Then you have to carry your kit around. Long gone are the days of sticking your bat into the side pocket of a small bag. This would end up making the rubber of the bat handle ride up showing string at one end and leaving you to have to chop the other end off due to excess grip at the top. Many clubbies of this era could have doubled up as rabbis. Oversized coffins became de rigueur amongst the cricketing fashionistas and were the cause of many a stubbed toe on your way in and out of the showers, but now the bag with wheels seems to be the luggage of choice.

Cricket kit is a strange thing. It can be lovingly looked after by some and scattered everywhere by others. You can tell a lot about an individual just by changing next to them. You can tell what sort of a person they are and in many cases how much money they earn. Some players even leave their kit all over the dressing room to return the following weekend to dirty whites. Others fold their clothes with neatness and order.

Cricket kit isn't cheap. A brand new, top-of-the-range bat can now cost over £500. For a whole kit bag of top-notch gear, you might need to take out a small mortgage just to get onto the field of play. Cricket equipment has changed. There's more choice, but the cost has gone up vastly when compared with what the average clubbie was earning 30 years ago.

Boots used to be fairly standard. Winit Worcesters were the cheap choice of the clubbie and you would see these in every club. The only problem with them was that the heel would come away from the sole. If you bought them new in April, by September you'd see a host of clubbies chasing balls to the boundary making flapping, clapping noises as they did so. I'm sure that counties don't need to give away clappers at T20 games like they do now but instead just need to recycle a load of Winit Worcester boots from the late 1980s! Now boots are better made and come in a variety of colours. The steel toe which saved many a batsman from crushing Yorkers also seems to be a thing of the past. These would double-up as great wear on a construction site for many a builder clubbie. On the down side, any clubbie who wore his Winit Worcesters to a night club on a Friday night would have been instantly refused entry.

Wicketkeeping gear is another thing that has changed. Pads would simply be batting pads –all keepers would wear them. Keeping pads of 30 years ago were wider than batting pads but with money being tighter back then, many clubbies would use the same ones they batted in. Even at club level now you often still see keeping pads that have been shorn off at the knee. Keeping gloves were generally just red in colour but now come in a multitude of shades. Our current 1st XI keeper has black, shiny ones that wouldn't look out of place on a dominatrix (although I have yet to see him take the field in a gimp mask with a gag ball in his mouth). Who knows what may happen in the future, given the way things are changing?

The helmet is a regular sight now in club cricket and are generally sported in the club colours. The days of Alec Stewart white ones are gone and they don't even get the comment 'Here comes Neil Armstrong' any more when a clubbie comes to the crease in one…

Gloves have become better and stronger and pads have become lighter. Shirts have become standard club ones with a badge on, often with a sponsor's name emblazoned across it and with some colour on the sleeves. The days of fielding in a Lyle and Scott top with a white, wide-brimmed sun hat seem to be a thing of the past. Baseball-style caps are now the 'in thing' and to see a Harlequin-style cap is as rare as a team staying behind after a match for seven or eight pints.

The contents of a cricket bag are constantly evolving and will no doubt be out of date by the time that you read this.

15
ARE STANDARDS DECLINING IN THE CLUB GAME?

Very occasionally, or perhaps every week depending on your club, you will play in a game of cricket that 'goes off'. These aren't good and as cricket becomes like Sunday morning football, unfortunately it is more common occurrence. I wrote the following article in *The Cricket Paper* in February 2016.

The decline of standards and behaviour in cricket has nosedived in recent years. Anyone who has played club cricket for a while will agree. In fact so much so that in April 2016 the MCC have decided to give umpires more powers to combat the problem from the 2017 season onwards. Cricketers could find themselves sent off or sin-binned as red and yellow cards will be introduced in university and club cricket as a trial, and it is hoped that the leagues will follow suit. If the proposed changes are deemed successful, then no doubt the professional game will implement the changes shortly afterwards. Four levels of offences will be trialled during the cricket season as those in the corridors of power clamp down on violence, racist behaviour, intimidation and a host of other problems that have crept into the game.

Five games were abandoned in the year of 2015 in club cricket due to fighting. In some cases police charges were brought against the culprits and in one game in recent years in a National Cup tie, the visiting Welsh supporters had a flag burned by those purporting to support the hosting English side as brawling broke out among the crowd. Players being hospitalised, criminal charges, people being hit with bats … put 'violence in club cricket' into a Google search and you will be shocked. Sledging between players instigated nearly all of the trouble, or the cricketing cheap shot, the sending-off of a batsman.

In the Saracens Hertfordshire Cricket League, where I have been known to ply my trade on occasion, more players were banned last year than in any other of the 31 years in which I have been playing.

Two of those have been given a *sine die* ban. Offences range from dissent to social media violations along with a plethora of other offences. In many cases a captain that fails to control his players will find his Saturday afternoon being spent anywhere but a cricket field, yet the problem seems to be getting worse.

The MCC have now had enough as they attempt to curb the excessive sledging and bad behaviour that causes the problem. Level Four offences, which include threatening an umpire, racist behaviour or assault of a player, official or spectator, are amongst the proposals that will constitute a red-card offence and see players sit out the rest of the game. If a batsman does it, he will be retired out.

Other sanctions that the MCC have proposed include a 'cooling-off' period in the sin bin for Level Three offences, such as bowlers slipping the batsman a deliberate beamer or intimidating behaviour towards an opposition player. Umpires will also have the powers to hand out five-run penalties for deliberate physical contact, such as shoulder barging, time wasting and dissent.

20 years ago these measures were put to the umpires at professional level, who refused, preferring to hand over disciplinary sanctions to match referees.

Having umpired many club games in recent years – none of which have broken out into a fight, may I hasten to add – the 'chirp' has been voluble and send-offs seem the norm. A send-off is the bowler continuing to spout verbal abuse, having dismissed a batsman. In boxing terms it is the equivalent of knocking out your opponent and then kicking him when the referee's count has reached ten. You've beaten your opponent, so why continue the battle when the war is won? In the 1990s, you might have got the occasional comment from a tired, cantankerous bowler on your way off, but these were few and far between and more amusing than the witless abuse served up by the modern-day club player.

So why have standards declined so alarmingly?

When I have written about money creeping into the game over the last few years, the feedback on social media seemed to think that the two were linked. There was a theory that players had so much more to lose and that the money that has crept into club cricket was reason behind the poor behaviour. That could be a possibility, but some of these games forced into abandonment were between two 4th XIs. I doubt they were being paid.

Generally club cricketers these days are younger. All-day cricket, pre-match warm-ups and increased travelling tends to rule out the family man in his 30s and the prominent demographic of many sides in club cricket is the under 25 sector. The calming presence of an older head is absent from many of these teams, as a premium is put on fitness and fielding.

Many of these teams don't even have the traditional after-match drink with the opposition any more, where problems that had arisen on the pitch were sorted out over a couple of pints. Even those who do stay for one will keep themselves in the clique of their own team mates as the younger generation have a quick energy drink before exiting the clubhouse. Lack of respect for the opposition, the umpires and the game is rife in club cricket.

This is a theory that was put to me by ex-Yorkshire, Gloucestershire and Somerset bowler Steve Kirby. No stranger to controversy himself during his playing days, a 20-year cricket career saw him direct some colourful quotes to the opposition. However, off the pitch Kirby is amiable, pleasant and one of the nicest people to play the sport that I have interviewed. He said, 'When I first started we'd have a few pints with the opposition and things would be sorted out. Towards the end of my career, we'd get back on the bus straight after the match and go, which was a shame as people would only see the idiot on the pitch and not the real person.' It's food for thought.

Whatever the reasons are, you just can't have the game descending into violence. There is a code of conduct for being a cricketer, even at club level, and I was always taught to respect your opposition, especially in away games when you are a guest in their clubhouse. The professional game also has a part to play; children watch the pros' every move and are influenced into copying the behaviour of their idols.

These standards seem to have slipped in recent years and the MCC has finally had enough. Haven't we all?

16

SIGHTSCREENS

Every club has someone that walks straight in front of a sightscreen. Whether it is a member of a public or a player who should know better it happens at every club in the land. Nothing gets up the nose more of an opening bowler more than a batsman who pulls away just as he has run in 30 yards. If you do this, expect to get a torrent of abuse or receive a Medusa-style glare from the bowler.

17
THE LIFE THAT YOU LEAD

Being a dedicated clubbie comes with its fair share of sacrifices. It starts at around 15 or 16 and ends when you die. Don't be sad – this is the life that we choose to lead, but it does come with a degree of detachment from the real world.

At 15 or 16 most boys suddenly discover the opposite sex. It dawns on the average 16-year-old that his penis isn't just for urinating with and he will spend his summer holidays at the local swimming pool trying (often unsuccessfully) to attract the girls from his class at school. For the junior clubbie, however, his Saturday afternoon in the summer is instead spent chasing a small piece of red leather around dusty cricket grounds, getting abuse from the opposition and sometimes his own team mates. No Saturday nights out for this youth at the cinema, as his is spent in the company of a 40-year-old divorcee moaning about the third lbw decision given against him in the last three weeks.

In your late teens and early 20s, the obsessed clubbie will find his career prospects have gone down the pan. Netting three times a week at university will take its toll on anyone and the realisation that you have gained only a third-class degree because you've used all your time playing, practicing and pissing it up with like-minded clubbies will only strike home as you are about to complete your studies. The fact that examination time is slap bang in the middle of the university cricket season is the bane of many an obsessed cricketer as he tries desperately to cram in the work that he should have been doing while at winter nets.

A mundane summer job is then taken so you can spend your winter in Australia only to get abused by clubbies down there for being a Pom, wafting outside of off stump or a host of other reasons as your technique is dissected like a laboratory rat. The crap money that this job pays you is invested in bats and into your cricket club bar should you decide that a winter being abused by Antipodeans isn't really your thing. While your university friends are getting their careers started on graduate schemes in the City, you find the biggest decision that you have to make is between Gray-Nicolls and Gunn & Moore. This is despite the fact that you bat at seven or eight.

In your later 20s, the obsession continues, despite fewer trips Down Under. Not being able to attend stag dos or having to say no to even family weddings because you have a top-of-the-table clash can lead to isolation from relatives and friends and it is not unknown for a clubbie to be written out of a rich relative's will. It is at this point that you are completely detached from the outside world. The refugee crisis of Syria means nothing to you as the only paperwork that you read will be the 2nd XI scorebook in the hope that the talented youngster down there doesn't nick your place in the 1sts.

The birth of clubbie children brings some slight relief and despite friends and relatives telling you that this is the most wonderful moment of your life, you find it comes a close second to grinding out a hundred on a damp wicket against a good bowling attack. You find yourself resenting the crying of your children when you need your sleep to prepare for a big game the following day. This is why the standard preparation for most clubbies involves nine or ten pints on a Friday night.

In your later 30s, your Mrs, who at this point is tired of cancelling engagements with friends due to your cricketing obsessive nature and divorces you, leading you to throw even more of your life into your cricket club. It is at this age that you realise that your cricket club will always love you, it will never have a headache, actually enjoys you staying in the bar until midnight and will never nag you. At this stage in life you'll find that your best mates tend to be around 20.

At work the clubbie is constantly thinking about his Saturday afternoon. Time spent on the station platform waiting for trains sees clubbies the world over perfecting 'air' forward defensives and prime selling time is spent on rival clubs' websites checking out the scores and recent results of upcoming opposition. You will know the opposition intimately due to the player profiles on their website yet should they pass you on the street, you wouldn't recognise them. However, you can quote their season's best verbatim and will have an intimate understanding of their strengths and weaknesses. You will even have worked out who they still have to play that season and spend vast amounts of time predicting their results against yours and where you will finish in the table. It is not unknown for clubbies to receive their P45 from their employer in this instance.

In his 40s the clubbie dreams and hopes of that one last day in the sun, that thought of a trial at county 2nd XI standard becomes a mere pipe dream. One more hundred, one last five-fer, one more diving catch is ever present in the mind of any self-respecting clubbie. In reality you spend every Saturday afternoon doing fine leg to fine leg as your fielding has gone. Despite this, your life is uplifted when your son finally reaches double figures in a colts game and the joy of him taking a wicket outweighs the petrol money spent ferrying him and his mates around various clubs in the locality. A wipe across the line for a midwicket four is worth sitting on a park bench on a freezing May night when the street lamps start to appear. You begin to live your cricket vicariously through your kid.

In your 50s the average clubbie turns to umpiring. Again, this brings with it a wealth of abuse from someone who is young enough to be your grandson. Despite the fact that you were in Baghdad when they were in their dad's bag, turning down an lbw from their quick bowler brings forth a stream of invective. It is at this age that most clubbies have at least two drink driving convictions under their belt.

In your 60s, the sheer volume of committee tasks weighs you down. You find that no one else is doing them around the club so you end up taking on far more than a recently retired person really should, all in the name of love for your cricket club. While your friends are spending their pensions on Saga holidays to Madeira, your summers are spent collecting glasses that have been left by junior members of the side in the outfield.

Your 70s are still filled with watching your club play, but you find that you don't recognise any of the players due to a mixture of Alzheimer's and the fact that nobody under 40 wants to speak to the cantankerous old sod in the pavilion. You sit with other like-minded ex-clubbies who you played with, supping half a bitter and moaning that things were far better in your day. You'll find as a clubbie that the longer that you have been retired, the better a player you were.

Finally you reach death. Your funeral fittingly will be held at a church near to your cricket club and the wake will be in your club bar. Like a sub-standard tea, a few curled-up sandwiches will be the only food on offer for the mourners. It will be attended en masse by a wealth of other clubbies from not only your club but rival clubs too. It turns out to be one of the best piss-ups of the season. Despite the fact that you have spent your whole life dishing out abuse and moaning about the players at your club, everyone says what a great bloke you were.

Three years after death all that is left are memories and your name on a plaque of a rotting bench that leans from side to side and has woodworm. This will be replaced when the next clubbie passes away.

This is the life of a clubbie.

18
THE BLOCKER

Throughout club cricket there will always be one individual who scores at a slower rate than his peers. The man who has more leaves than a eucalyptus tree, more blocks than Legoland and sees out more maidens than a convent, this person is a stalwart of club cricket.

Across the land this man has ruined many a decent game of cricket. Preferring not to lose than to go for the win, he will end up at 25 not out after 40 overs and be satisfied with his day's work. He will have a decent average due to the number of 'red inkers' that he accumulates over the season but watching him pot out yet another draw is the cricketing equivalent of the offside trap. Effective – yes, interesting – no.

This person will be full of excuses, telling you that the bowling was decent and that he had to be watchful, when in reality he has played a forward defensive to donkey drop bowler, who was only brought on by the opposition skipper in a bid to try to open the game up. Whatever the skipper does, this bloke plays a forward defensive and any runs he does actually manage to accumulate come from shots that would be dot balls to normal batsmen, except that the field is all crowded around the bat, thus allowing him a precious single.

With the advent of T20 coming into Sunday cricket this person will soon be a thing of the past. My childhood was spent with many a clubbie like this.

Every cricket club has a blocker.

19
JUG AVOIDANCE

Over a summer in England you will hear these words often. In fact, Jack Brooks mentions it in the foreword as an integral part of his childhood. Every weekend there are jug avoiders throughout the land and there are some serial offenders.

To set the scene, in club cricket in the south of England you are required to buy a jug of beer for your team mates should you reach 50 or 100, take five wickets or three catches in a match. Being out for 49, 99 or bowling a load of tripe at the number eleven when you are on four wickets, would be deemed as jug avoidance. The difference of scoring one run between 49 and 50 can save you £15 or so in the bar later. In the north of England, it is different. I believe that in the Lancashire League you get a 'collection' from the watching crowd if you reach a milestone, but in the south you have to pay for your success.

The author of this book is a serial jug avoider. I don't mean to be. I have had five scores in the 90s since my last hundred. I didn't actually want the umpire at Winchmore Hill to 'saw me off' on 99 when the ball hit my thigh pad, let me tell you. However, I will hold my hands up to ending up 98 not out in a game a few years ago. I was on 92 when my opening partner potted out a maiden of unbelievable buffet bowling in the hope that I would score my two fours to win the game, when we needed just six to win. Having been given a full toss, my scream of anguish could be heard for miles around as I hit it too well, the ball sailing over the rope as I ended up on 98 not out with us winning the game by ten wickets. On two other occasions, I have tamely chipped to cover in the 90s.

Many clubbies have avoided the jug over the years. Running themselves out seems to be the avoidance of choice, although I have seen people get deliberately stumped, too. The experienced jug avoider will pat full tosses back in the hope of grabbing a single to end up on 48 not out instead of smashing the thing to the boundary.

I have seen many a clubbie refuse to buy a jug. A non-drinking Indian who I played with in the 1980s would regularly be chided for not getting his jug in. His response of 'I only buy orange juice' or 'I only get them for tons' would cut no ice with his teenage team mates.

The culture of the jug is something that is not seen so often these days in club cricket. I cover the subject elsewhere in the book but it is a great form of team bonding and it should be continued. The jug is a way of congratulating your team mate by drinking all of his beer, although the jug should be shared amongst opponents, too. In fact, it is good etiquette to take it around the opposition first.

Jug avoidance rears its head in many forms and ways. It happens most weekends and most importantly, it is an integral part of club cricket.

20
THE TOUR

One thing all club cricketers have to experience is the club tour. This is a chance to get away from work, play cricket for a week and generally return a broken man. Nothing brings on early cirrhosis quite like a club tour and if you play a side on a Saturday after they return from tour, it normally results in a victory. For the side who haven't been on tour, despite them playing all week, having their eye in is the last thing on their mind as their focus will be on the barmaid who served them all week.

It doesn't matter where you tour. It may be a few months Down Under or a week in a seedy B&B in a run-down UK seaside resort, the club cricket tour means one thing: bad behaviour from responsible adults who should know better.

Whether you're an international representing your country or a clubbie stepping out from your mate's rusty automobile that has just about made it from the metropolis to the dank seaside resort where you've decamped for a week, the phrase 'what goes on tour, stays on tour' will be heard at regular intervals throughout the week. For the uninitiated this is roughly translated as, 'Do not tell my Mrs that I slept with the barmaid.'

Freed from the shackles of work and domestic duties, cricketers are renowned for letting their hair down. Aided by copious alcohol consumption. they get into scrapes that, frankly, would take some serious explaining if they ever became public knowledge. Whilst this isn't just confined to cricketers (just ask any touring rugby team or numerous football teams on pre-season jollies), it seems from the tales that I have heard over the years that those who play cricket have batted above their average when it comes to tour escapades.

Now the bad behaviour on tour I am referring to can take place both on and off the field and at any level from the international arena to the annual club mid-season trip. The 1980s tours of England were famous – or infamous, depending on your point of view. Stories of

Ian Botham partying, England cricketers having a smoke of illicit substances, the list went on. Often ladies were planted by the tabloid press, a move noticed by David Gower when England were playing 'up country' in Australia. Suddenly two rather attractive ladies with strong Eastern European accents appeared, offering the cricketers more than a crash course in the Estonian or Latvian language. Luckily for Gower and Co. they said 'Nyet' before they became the victims of a red-top sting.

Ironically, on the same tour other ladies were planted in a hotel but with the cricketers opting for an early night it was the tabloid paper's own cricket correspondent who got amorous, leaving red-faced red-top editors back in London fuming with their scribe.

The club tour will necessitate sleeping with a team mate as most rooms are shared. This is essential for the goodwill of the tour and is all about team bonding. Except that there will always be two who are left at the end. Often this will be one gentleman who is there for the cricket and one who is there for the après cricket. Many a story has arisen from those on tour going down for breakfast whilst his new room mate is coming in from the previous night's excursions. Philip Clive Roderick Tufnell would regularly have to bribe hotel receptionists and bell boys to smuggle him back into his room. Ian Botham and David Gower both banned Graham Gooch from going for his early-morning runs as they would often cross paths the following dawn.

Other tour shenanigans are often played out on the pitch. Your hosts, having taken a day off work to play you, will want a serious game of cricket. To be greeted by 13 sleep-deprived blokes reeking of booze and having a row about who will start off the umpiring is not their idea of great fun.

There are many other tour japes that happen to foster disharmony among team mates. One ex-team mate of mine who was woken up in the middle of the night by his so called 'friends' pouring an ice-cold glass of water over him as he lay fast asleep in his bed wasn't overly impressed by the bonding exercise employed by his chums. So much so that it nearly caused a fight.

On a club cricket tour we advise always respecting the rules, customs and values of your hosts. In a hotel in Somerset our welcoming host asked us politely to avoid a certain part of the hotel which was occupied by his elderly guests. This we complied with until a 3.00am drinking session got the better of one of our party. Much to the manager's chagrin, two of his octogenarian guests were woken in the middle of the night to see one of our team mates walking down the corridor completely naked apart from his bat, cap, pads, thigh pad and box. Breakfast was slightly frosty the following morning.

Another piece of advice is never, ever put your name down to be the tour leader. You will find yourself playing the diplomat and constantly apologising to the hotel manager for your team mates' behaviour the previous night. A friend of mine – Tim Grover – would regularly organise tours to Hastings for our club. Having been banned from one hotel the previous year he organised a stay at a caravan park. A note was pushed through the door the following morning requesting to see Tim in the manager's office due to the excessive noise.

Unfortunately Tim himself was sleeping off the previous night's excesses so one of our party took it upon himself to pretend to be Tim to the manager. Apologetic and sincere, this was being sorted with utmost diplomacy in the office, until 15 minutes later in walked the real Tim Grover and introduced himself. To say that the manager of the campsite was unhappy with the imposter is an understatement. It turned out to be one of those 'I'm Spartacus' moments. Needless to say, we found ourselves having to find alternative accommodation yet again the following year.

There are other legendary tales which have done the rounds of cricket clubs around my locality, but they could well be urban myths. I've heard stories of a hotel in Somerset laying on a particularly warm reception for a side from North-West London, but their visitors made things far warmer, however, by setting fire to one of the rooms they were occupying, leading to the hotel proprietor urgently dialling 999. Needless to say their reservation for the following summer was politely declined.

Most tours don't end up with a frantic call to the emergency services and run fairly smoothly, albeit ending up with a bevy of broken individuals by the end of the week. However, if you are inclined to get involved in such japes and tomfoolery just remember the old adage, 'what goes on tour, stays on tour.'

I'd recommend every clubbie goes on one at some point in his life.

21
DRIVING

A few years ago, a rival side were playing another team in our league when on arrival at the ground, their skipper and star batsman drove his car into the pavilion while trying to reverse park. The crunch of metal and the broken rear lights were noticed by many of the home side. When he came in to bat one of the fielders shouted out to his opening bowler, 'Come on mate, pitch the ball up and let's get him driving. We know he's rubbish at that!'

22
THE AGEING CRICKETER

Sometimes as a clubbie you will be called back to play a game, despite protesting that you retired years ago. Shortness of availability, a President's Day or just fancying it again after a few years away can be the reason. My mate John Thorp wrote the following after coming back to play a couple of years ago and it was a painful experience for him.

Cricket is a young man's game, so they say, and with me about to enter my 43rd year in a few weeks, it has to be said that every season is getting harder and harder. I know some players, even professionally, have gone on for years. Well they're fit, and I'm not. So there.

This is what happens to us club players, where the malaise starts in your mid- to late 30s. We have a reasonably long career at 1st team level, 18 years in my case, and then you find yourself dropped to the 2nds. At 2nd XI level what you really want are the youngsters who think they are quick but spray it more than your average porn star, where the slightest touch goes through a similarly elderly slip and gulley cordon, providing you flash hard enough.

What you invariably end up facing are similar-aged bowlers, who you've played against for years, and therefore know where you hit it. These dibbly-dobblers, actually require you to hit the ball on these early-season wickets, and with some smart-arsed keeper standing up due to their lack of pace, the chances of you getting to the pitch of the ball landing just back of a length are slimmer than Posh Spice.

Therefore, all that's going to happen is it'll go Rod Hull (aerial), and normally to mid-on or mid-off. Alternatively, you can use your cunning and experience and pat the old sod back for ten overs, before losing your patience, especially on these slow tracks, and hitting one to mid-on or mid-off. Your third option is trying to smash him out of the attack, before ultimately hitting one down the throat of, yes you've guessed it, mid-on or mid-off. The final option, and one I have become familiar with this year is hitting the ball on the deck to mid-on or mid-off, calling for the single due to being strangled on slow tracks by said seamers, before finally realising that being the fat, unfit bastard that I am, trying to run 22 yards is akin to watching Rik Waller on that *Celebrity Boot Camp* programme the other year. Similar to Rik, I am soon back in the pavilion in tears looking for sympathy.

The other thing that goes is your fielding. Playing with guys who are in the early 20s, and at the top of their fielding game, they don't realise that you were like them once upon a time, and were half-reasonable in the field. Batsmen now take you on as the old boy in the side, and what was once a reasonable arm, comes through as quick as a Jeremy Snape delivery in T20! It can be a cruel game.

So what happens is, you end up in the 3rd XI as your batting and fielding aren't quite up to standard, where you can maybe hold out for another ten years. Or you can retire, but that's not for me. Cricket for me is an addiction. It is to me what booze was to George Best, what a gram of coke was to Amy Winehouse, or what a team mate's wife is to John Terry. I can't help it. I want to play, or at least be involved in my club, and for that reason I will always be an old fool. The flame slowly dying, but I'm still having a bloody good laugh as it slowly burns out. There's no fool, quite like an old fool. I'm sure there are plenty out there who can sympathise?

23
THE SHIDAS TOUCH

Every club cricketer will at some point go through a barren patch.
Like a starvation diet or a camel storing up water and fat in its hump
for a long trek through the desert, the club cricketer only has the
memories of a decent knock the previous year. As in the case of
King Midas, who back in the day was known for everything he
touched turning to gold, the run of low scores is known as 'The
Shidas Touch'. It is where everything you touch turns to shite.
Whatever you do, you find a way of getting out.

The run of low scores is hard to take. This is when the ribbing of
one's team mates tends to grate and there will invariably be talk of
giving up the game. This is the point of no return. The moment
where you do not know where your next run is coming from and
despite the fact that you might be wealthy, you just cannot buy a run.

I am fully aware of this from personal experience. In the 1990
season I started off with a first-ball duck. By the end of May I had
failed to trouble the scorer six times. I was considering changing my
name to Whiting 0 as that was what was being recorded in the
scorebook so often. You go from being philosophical about it, to
angry, to wanting to smash your stumps down, back to philosophical
before just laughing about it. Then in the privacy of the dressing
room you just want to smash the room to smithereens.

Another colleague at my club had the misfortune of being out twice
for a duck against the same bowler in two days. Not only that but
both dismissals were in the opening over and the same manner of
dismissal – caught behind. Both snares were via the cut shot.

Another chap I know from club cricket played on a Bank Holiday
weekend on a Saturday, Sunday and on the Monday. He got three
ducks in three days, two of them of the golden variety. This was in
the middle of a drought period for him where he registered six ducks
in a row. And he was a number three bat!

Other misfortunes have befallen decent players. One of the bloggers on my website, John Thorp, was a good batsman who scored 1,600 runs in one season. The following year saw him amass just over 200 and that included a century in one of the games.

As a child I played representative cricket with someone who later became a professional cricketer. He was once found crying and snivelling behind the pavilion after registering a duck. Disappointed with himself for failing his ever-present, dominant mother, he couldn't contain hold it in any longer and was in floods of tears.

Low scores affect us all. Many a player I have known has retired or gone over to playing golf after a run like this. Many have taken solace in alcohol, while a string of ex-clubbies can be found looking very bored in garden centres on a weekend after a season of this. There is no reason why it happens. Well, sometimes it's because the player is crap, and sometimes technical faults creep in, but remember – whatever happens – as Tony Blair and New Labour told us, things can only get better.

24
LOSING YOUR TEMPER

During a run of low scores many club cricketers lose their temper. Normal, responsible adults – frustrated by a combination of a boss shouting at them all week, a wife nagging them all week, a mundane job or lack of sex – can snap after a dodgy lbw decision or playing a rash shot come the weekend. Every club cricketer across the land has lost his temper at some point whether it is within the sanctuary of the dressing room or al fresco and in view of 30 or so members of the public. We advise never to laugh at this point.

I have seen many cricketers lose the plot. I have seen varying degrees of such plot-losing, too. Some batsmen, when they are out, merely take off their gloves and pads. Others launch their kit around the room. It is at this point that all openers are grateful for their place in the order as they never have to pad up while a tornado of kit is hurled around my some poor sod who's just been sawed off by the opposition bent umpire.

It isn't just club cricketers either. Mike Gatting once put his fist through a pane of glass at Lord's after an lbw decision went down like a bad lunch with the ex-Middlesex skipper. Matt Prior, at the same ground, bounced his bat off of the dressing room sofa and straight through a window, showering the elderly members of the MCC below with shards of glass. It nearly caused one or two to choke on their gin and tonics. Ben Stokes once had to leave a tour after punching a locker in the West Indies, while Jack Brooks told me that his team mate at Northamptonshire, the ex-South African international Andrew Hall, had a 'special bat' that came out of the locker specifically to beat seven shades of crap out of various items in the dressing room. Radiators, benches, lockers … nothing was safe. He'd use his special bat in order not to smash up his real ones after either a low score or a rough decision.

It is often the send-off that can lead to such violence. A send-off is basically a cheap shot. At club level throughout the land, every weekend, having already beaten your man, a 'tata' or 'thanks for coming' from the slip cordon can result in criminal damage, while a 'don't use up all the hot water in the shower, son', is often the precursor to some serious structural redevelopment of cricket pavilions.

Some don't even wait to reach the hutch. I have personally witnessed people throw their bat all the way back to the pavilion often launching it javelin-style three or four times on that long and lonely walk back. I have seen another chap at our club kick his helmet all the way back, occasionally picking it up to launch it back towards the turf. The smashed helmet still takes pride of place in our bar, a grisly reminder of that day and like a macabre museum exhibit. Think of the famous *Fawlty Towers* scene when Basil's car broke down and he proceeded to hit it repeatedly with a branch – this'll give you some idea of what cricketers are like during this walk back.

Then you have the others who smash stumps. I think at all times we have wanted to smash the stumps out of the ground when dismissed, but most of us refrain from doing so as it goes against the Spirit of Cricket. I have it happen seen over the years and it varies from a little tap in frustration to a full-blown mow, like a farmer with a scythe removing all three stumps out of the ground in one fell swoop. Even in the professional game Chris Broad, ex-England opening bat and father of current international Stuart, did this in Australia once. Not only that but he had 130-odd to his name at the time. If I got a 130 for England I'd be doing cartwheels. Broad is now a match referee in the international arena. I kid you not.

As with Stokes, losing your temper can often cause a self-inflicted injury. Putting your fist through a glass window isn't the brightest of ideas and it is not unknown for a bat to bounce back at someone off a dressing room bench boomerang-style, hitting them in the face. Team mates padding up can also be at risk of flying bats.

Some players just sit there with their pads on for an hour or so. Others can be distraught. Often a number eleven when out can be heartbroken as when he is out there is a finality to it. It's the last wicket and the game is over. He often thinks he himself has lost the game, when in reality it's the batsmen above him who haven't got enough runs. Others I have seen over the years have a little blub, a little snivel and get on with it. Yes, these are grown men.

I've seen captains go absolutely bonkers in dressing rooms. I have seen sides locked in for an hour after a game because the batting has failed, or the bowler's bowled badly or the side dropped too many catches. I have seen bowlers slip in a deliberate beamer having lost the plot and I have witnessed a captain getting a bowler to bowl one. A few years ago in the international game we witnessed a West Indian bowler run through the crease and throw one at a South African batsman from around 16 yards.

From the teapot-style of a captain with his hands on his hips to players throwing down their caps in disgust, cricket is a game of high emotions. Ranging from elated to downright incandescent with rage, a dressing room can be a harbour of the extremes. It doesn't matter if you play the game professionally or like most of us, for a village Sunday 3rd XI, you will see a temper tantrum at some point during the season. Sometimes you see two or three in one day.

Just be wary of the flying bats and my advice is not to say a word to the incoming bat. Even a good-natured 'bad luck mate' is likely to be returned with 'no bad luck about it, it was a shit shot/bad decision/the moon was at a certain angle' (delete as applicable).

Cricket is a funny old game.

25
THE WIFE

A club who play in Gloucestershire told me a story of the wife of one of their team members who turned up to watch a game of cricket. Not normally seen at the ground and not an avid cricket lover she attempted to make polite conversation with the female scorer. After 20 overs of the first innings she asked 'Who's winning?' The lads nearby just smiled politely and said, 'Hmm not sure.' This has happened in every club across the land.

26
ONE IN THE BOX

Generally at the start of the season and during one of your first times out in the middle, you will hear a sound that you often hear at this time of year. No, not bat on ball and not the clatter of stumps, although I have heard the latter on many an occasion. Think of a medium-pace seamer nibbling it back in late to the batsman on a green wicket and the thud of the ball into the batsman's box. When some people think of the sounds of an English spring they think of lambs bleating, maybe a cuckoo, but not for me… Nothing more exemplifies this time of year than that unmistakeable cadence of cork on cricketing cock.

When I was a lad, I was taught by an Australian at under-11 level, and it was he who taught us that it should be the first thing we put on. He said that if we didn't, we would all be singing like the bloke off 'The Lion Sleeps Tonight' by Tight Fit. The box has come on a lot in recent years, these days being of more durable plastic than the lightweight pink things that were shoved down there in the 1970s. They even had holes in them, and if facing anyone quick these tended to force the plastic back and skin through the vents causing more misery than if your crown jewels had been left unguarded.

Another coach I had would get us to remember to put a box in by recalling a game that he played in the early 1970s. One batsman wasn't wearing a protector and was hit in the nether regions. He hit the deck fairly sharply and stayed there for a good 10 minutes. When play finally resumed, the tears had been wiped away and he had been offered to retire hurt, but he continued. Two balls later (pardon the pun) he was hit in the same place and they had to carry the poor chap off.

Two Accringtonians recall marvellous stories of being hit in such regions with David Lloyd getting hit by Jeff Thomson, who was slinging it down at around 99mph in 1975, and then Graeme Fowler getting hit by Joel Garner at Lord's in 1984. Fowler described this to me once over a pint after a commentary for Test Match Sofa, now known as Guerilla Cricket. I winced and yelped at every sentence. Having been hit by the big man about 5 minutes before lunch, his box was in bits and he waited for all of his team mates to leave the dressing room before he could check whether he needed to visit the local infirmary. Luckily, the box hadn't circumcised him, but The Fox will never forget the day when Garner fractured his genital guard. I'm still in pain just typing this out and recalling him telling me the story, and no, you haven't got your webcam on but I can see every one of you wincing as they read this.

Bumble, meanwhile, copped one in his Lancashire hotpot from the quickest bowler in the world. With ventilation holes being of a fashion back then as well as being a useful way to keep the flies away from your Vegemite sandwich in Australia, Bumble's meat and two veg were forced at great velocity through his codpiece. Watching Bumble hit the deck reminded me of a South American footballer looking for a penalty.

There are different ways though of getting hit and each brings its own pain in various ways. Firstly, there's the spinner. Yep, it doesn't even have to be travelling that quickly to do damage. Sometimes while sweeping, if you don't get the front pad in the way, it can hit you on the bottom of the box, pushing everything up. This tends to be the delayed pain where you think you are OK, and then just as the bowler is trotting in for his next delivery, an overwhelming feeling which is a hybrid of wanting to be sick and impending torrential diarrhoea takes over.

Then there's getting hit flush on. This can push things back into the body. This is more of an immediate pain than the previous type, but still takes the wind out of your sails, as the impact of plastic back into your 'Shaun Pollocks' hits home. Then there is the trapping of scrotum, which has found its way out of the plastic casing as you have just run a three. This tends to be more of a nipping pain, often causing bruising to ones sac and any protestations to your Mrs that you did it while playing cricket, fall on deaf ears, thus ruining not only your Saturday night, but also your week/month/year/life – delete as applicable.

The thing about getting boxed is you know it is coming. You know that the ball has beaten you having nipped back and you know it's going to hit. The only thing you don't know is how much it's going to hurt. Sometimes you get away with it, and other times you don't. Getting boxed is a lottery, like batting at Sabina Park in 1998 or picking a touring squad to Australia in 2013.

The acoustics of ball on box reverberate around the ground often accompanied by a Monica Seles-type grunt. Everyone on the pitch thinks it is hilarious apart from the poor sod who's been hit, desperately trying to catch his breath, like an asthmatic at altitude. There will always be some comedian in the fielding side, and no matter what he says, it is never funny. The old classics like 'don't rub 'em, count 'em' are trotted out, and you know the batsman's OK when he asks if 'the pain can be taken away, but leave the swelling'.

Getting hit in the box, however, is never a laughing matter.

27
MY DAUGHTER

My 15-year-old daughter Hannah has never shown a huge interest in our summer game despite her twin brother being obsessed with it. One day, I took her to watch and had to answer various questions about the game. One was, 'Why is there sawdust on the pitch? Has someone been sick or something?' This was followed up by 'he's broken the sticks' as a batsman got bowled. 'I saw two little bits of wood fly off.' Yes, I know it's my fault for not educating her earlier in life. Every club will have someone like this who turns up at some point in the season.

28
THE COMMITTEE

Ever wonder how your club is run? Or who runs it? Who makes the decisions? Who is responsible for the extra strong lager behind the bar that results in numerous cry-offs on a Sunday morning? Very occasionally you'll see people who turn up in suits all congregate around a table in your clubhouse. Gone are the kids in skater shorts to be replaced by old guys drinking bitter and talking in far less audible volume than the usual suspects on a Saturday night. This is your cricket committee.

A cricket committee depends on the constitution of your club. All clubs will have club rules. It may be run by one person, someone power-crazed like Genghis Khan. It might even be, like a few clubs are starting to become, outsourced. In general, though, it is run by the committee who are voted in by the members every year at an AGM.

Here's your lowdown as to what these individuals do:

The President – or El Presidente as he will be referred to in most clubs. Apart from having a game normally played for the benefit of him and his friends once a year during cricket week, he doesn't really do a lot. A president is a figurehead for the club and it is an honour to have this position. Presidents rarely sit on the committee, yet are often asked to stump up the air fare for the new overseas player. Of course it helps if your president is stinking rich as the quality of overseas player that you get tends to be better. If you see a red-faced bloke in the bar and he is not the groundsman, he will be the president. While the groundsman will have red cheeks due to the amount of time he spends outdoors, the flushed cheeks of El Presidente tend to be due to his liking for the strong stuff. He tends to drink a lot.

The Chairman – if the president is a club figurehead then this man holds the power as he's usually behind the decision making of the committee. Think of the president as the Queen and the chairman as the Prime Minister. Often a worried man with the stresses and strains of the club on his shoulders, he makes the club captain look positively carefree. This bloke needs diplomacy skills aplenty, often being the public face of the club at events. The chairman needs to run the club's activities both on and off the field as well as leading the committee. To combat the stress, he tends to drink a lot.

The Treasurer – this guy is the George Osborne of the club, the Chancellor of the Exchequer. Trying to get money out of him for expenses and necessary club kit is hard enough, let alone a drink. Graphs and Excel spreadsheets accompany him to most meetings and he will always stress how we must not spend too much despite the club bringing in a GDP that would put a third-world country to shame. Often prudent, some treasurers are known to drive very expensive cars. Whether this has come out of club funds or if these individuals are as careful with their own finances as they are with your cricket club's is for you to decide. Rarely drinks.

The Press Secretary – this guy's role has changed in recent years from scribbling a match report on a beer mat and phoning it in to the local press, to being in charge of the club's website. Editorial skills are needed to remove the captain's report of a dodgy lbw so he doesn't get a ban from the league. The press sec is the online face of the club and it is a very important role to play in the club. He will be the Alistair Campbell, the spin doctor of the committee.

The Secretary – types up minutes, collates addresses and organises the whole thing brilliantly. The secretary will often be seen clutching either a laptop or numerous sheets of paper, depending on his IT skills. Often seen in the background, he performs an extremely valuable function for your club and the whole thing would go to pot without this person. The Denis Thatcher of every cricket club, although whether he has Denis' predilection for a gin and tonic is entirely dependent on the culture of your club. So yes, probably.

The Honorary Team Secretary – the Lord Lucan of every club because no one in their right mind wants the job. Therefore it falls to the captain in most clubs. The role requires you to find out the availability of all players across the club and ensure that they turn up on a Saturday or Sunday afternoon. It's enough to turn most sane individuals to drink, drugs and a host of other anti-social behaviour, which is why this role remains vacant in the honours list of most clubs I know.

The Fixture Secretary – this person is busy all winter and sits on their arse all summer – if they've done their job properly. He or she is responsible for ensuring that the fixture takes place and needs careful liaison with other clubs' fixture secs. This can go wrong with spectacular results, either meaning that you are all changed and ready to go out without an opposition to play, or, even better, when two opposition XIs turn up at your ground. Good fixture secs will always blame the opposition when there is an administrative cock-up. The fixture sec can often go into hiding at this point and changes his telephone number. The John Stonehouse of the club.

The Colts Secretary – many clubs are dressing this role up as Director of Cricket or the like. The colts sec is a Pied Piper, often followed by a host of screaming kids. He carries out a vital role in the club, ensuring that there is a stream of talent coming through to fill your XIs when your average clubbie gets too old. The colts sec is responsible for the education of many a child until he reaches the age of 18 and starts drinking with less responsible members of your club. The Michael Gove of club cricket.

The Bar Secretary – he is a very important person who is behind the running of a cricket club bar. In fact, some would say the most crucially important person within the whole organisation. This person brings vital funds in to every cricket club across the country and his job often requires him to close the premises at 3.00am. Bleary-eyed, constantly tired, often grumpy due to lack of sleep and generally getting a load of abuse as he curtails the Saturday-night drinking of a load of degenerates who have had more than enough already. This man often does the jobs of the committee that no one else has any inclination to do such as clearing up the vomit of the younger members of the side or unblocking toilets. The Jeremy Hunt of every cricket club.

The Welfare Officer – most clubs now have to have a welfare officer responsible for the wellbeing of junior cricketers. This is done so that they can reach Clubmark accreditation and receive large amounts of funding from various bodies. The welfare officer is often a woman and her glare can stop a man at twenty paces should she hear inappropriate language in the club bar. The same can be said for certain songs that permeate clubhouses the length and breadth of the country on a Saturday night. Both of the above are regular occurrences in many cricket clubs. The Angela Merkel of the club.

Auditors – who are these people? What do they do? They are in the constitution of every cricket club yet no one knows them from Adam, let alone what they are there for. They are actually there to stop the treasurer from running off with club funds, to stop grants for kids' cricket ending up in the pockets of the chairman and to stop people being naughty with cricket club money. Err, that's about it really. A junior back bencher in cricket committee terms.

In addition to the above you will have the captains who are covered elsewhere in the book, various hangers-on and general drunks at the bar earwigging into conversations that should be confined to the committee. This is the powerhouse of every cricket club.

29
THE CRICKET CLUB DOG

As Jack Brooks mentioned in the foreword of the book, cricket clubs are wonderful environments to raise children in. However, virtually every club across the land has a resident dog. My dog Moses is a chocolate Labrador and has raided many a tea that an unsuspecting player has put on the ground. His finest hour – taking an ice cream out of the hands of a toddler – didn't exactly endear me to the parents. He is terrified of our tea lady who shouts at him whenever he goes anywhere near the kitchen and just longingly gazes at the goodies that have been put out for the players.

Dogs come in all colours, shapes and sizes – a bit like us clubbies – and their feeding habits are also of a similar nature.

Once a year I visit Hertford Cricket Club to play a game in their cricket week and there is a resident chocolate Labrador there who roams the outfield. Brilliantly, this dog has been trained not to cross the boundary rope, although I did spot it once wandering across the sightscreen behind the bowler's arm.

Another dog, a Border Collie who spent time at our cricket club in the 1990s, used to catch cricket balls in his mouth that its owner would hit 40 or 50 yards with a cricket bat. The clunk of the ball on tooth enamel as he caught it would send shivers down the spines of most veterinary surgeons and, on closer inspection, a front row of chipped teeth adorned this canine's mouth.

One batsman I played with used to hit boundary flags or anything else that was close by on the way off in a show of frustration at a poor shot, although I noticed that he didn't do this at one Hertfordshire ground that had a sleeping Rottweiler next to the away dressing room. His water bowl remained intact.

A cricket dog can have its uses too. A ball that lands in the middle of a patch of stinging nettles is not one that many fielders will volunteer to search for, but the dog has no fear. He will go and retrieve it far quicker, thus not holding up the game for long. That is, if he decides to give it back. Retrieving it is one thing, but giving it back is a completely different kettle of fish for the cricket dog. A cricket dog can also be useful if the ball does get lost. A quick chew from a Mastiff on one side of the ball and you will find that reverse swing suddenly comes into the fray. Man's best friend and definitely an opening bowler's.

It isn't just the dogs that inhabit the clubs. Neighbouring gardens can be the worst nightmare for a clubbie fielder who has to venture into them to go and collect the ball. One of our number was once chased out of a garden by the might of a Jack Russell but on hearing the bark of a larger dog, many clubbies will give up the ghost and call for a spare ball instead.

Other animals have been known to reside in cricket clubs, too. Unfortunately one poor hedgehog died having got stuck in our netting and having been part of the food chain of a variety of North London's fauna, none of the boys wanted to take responsibility for untangling poor 'Sonic' and putting him in the bin. Eventually he rotted away, and the option of recycling him as one of the elderly members' batting gloves was not taken up.

At Highgate Cricket Club in the 1980s the groundsman would save his energy and instead of mowing the pitch, he would employ his three or four goats to keep the outfield short. At Bayford CC, I pulled out of a delivery as a darting swallow whizzed past my head. Meanwhile many clubs play host to angry wasps' nests that tend to ruin the post-match lager. In wet weather it isn't unusual for ducks to become resident on the temporary lakes of cricket grounds and even this season after a ball went into bushes for a boundary, it was followed by a squawking moorhen and her young family running off at speed in the other direction. Foxes have been known to raid post-match barbecues, and all clubbies who play at a ground near water will have been bitten by cricket club mosquitoes.

A cricket club dog might be responsible for holding up play by running across the pitch, or causing the groundsman to remove one of its turds from on a length, but dogs and cricket clubs go together. It is a safe environment for them and they are part of the summer.

Long live the clubbie hound.

30
THE YIPS

Very occasionally you'll be playing club cricket at quite a decent standard and it all goes wrong for someone on the pitch. You wonder how they have been selected at such a level and then realise that they have just lost it. Run-ups, actions, the ability to release the ball – nothing seems to work. This is known as the Yips and it's a sad sight to see. Yes, even when it happens to that bloke who has gobbed off at you and questioned your technique for a number of seasons. Well … perhaps not, but it's still not good to see any of your team mates have to suffer them.

The Yips are quite possibly the worst thing to happen to any cricketer. Occasionally this will happen to the poor clubbie. A decent bowler will suddenly just lose the plot. Think how you cringed at Simon Kerrigan in the final Ashes game a few years ago, or felt for poor Scott Boswell in the final at Lord's in 2001 as he delivered delivery after delivery that couldn't hit the mark. Imagine a porn star getting herpes, a pianist losing his fingers or a fluffer getting a cold sore – the yips in cricket is far worse!

How do I know this? Because it has happened to me. A promising spinner in my early 20s averaging 50 to 60 wickets a season in 1st XI cricket, all of a sudden I just couldn't pitch the thing. I served up head-high beamers followed double bouncers and with my team mates looking at me as if I'd turned up to play pissed, I just wanted to get the over finished as quickly as I could before praying the skipper would take me off. The 1980s boy band Brother Beyond summed it up in their famous song 'The harder I try, the further away from me it's slipping'.

I now don't bowl at all, and one friend, our former wicketkeeper, has only just started talking to me again after 15 years when I bowled one of the beamers so slowly in an effort to get it right, that the batsman middled a pull into his jaw from a yard away resulting in three lost teeth and a lifetime of gingivitis-related gum trouble!

It has happened to far higher-profile cricketers than me and on far bigger stages than the Hertfordshire Cricket League. Scott Boswell, having played in the semi-final of the Cheltenham & Gloucester Trophy in 2001 and whipped out four Lancashire and England players, must have been delighted to have been selected for the final. His first over was actually OK – if you can call dropping it short and getting cut for four OK – but then, bowling at the left-handed Marcus Trescothick, he suddenly went to pieces. He basically couldn't hit the cut strip on either side of the wicket. Panicking, he delivered a 14-ball over including 8 wides. Even his run-up went and he retired from the first-class game soon after that episode.

A recent interview in 2014 in the *Guardian* by Andy Bull revealed that he came back in club cricket and bowled a 28-ball over, the poor sod!

So what are the yips? We've all, no doubt, come up against some bastard at lower XI cricket who sprays it like Ron Jeremy in the final scene of most of his films, before pitching one on middle and leg and nipping it away, clipping the top of your off stump. That is not the yips. The yips are losing your ability to pitch the ball, losing your run-up or even losing the ability to let the ball go, resulting in head-high beamers or the type of delivery that look like something from Barnes Wallis's drawing board.

It seems to happen most often to slow left-armers. Twirly man Keith Medlycott was picked for an England tour thanks to some fine performances for his county, but 18 months later retired after not being able to even release the ball in a game for Surrey 2nd XI. Phil Edmonds was another who bowled off one pace in an effort to combat this ghastly affliction. Norman Gifford also had spells where he bowled triple-bouncing daisy cutters and Gavin Hamilton, while not one of this breed of bowler, was another who struggled in his later career. Gladstone Small bowled a horrendous 18-ball over for Warwickshire once, no-balling left, right and centre and littered with wides. His skipper, Geoff Humpage, allegedly commented, 'We wanted three quick overs from him before lunch. We just didn't realise they would all be bowled in one go.' Suddenly you go from bowling like Shaun Pollock to bowling a load of bollocks and for no discernible reason.

It can happen in other sports, too. Golfers such as Bernhard Langer suddenly faced with a 6-inch putt would tap it an inch, snooker players like Stephen Hendry just shove the ball a couple of inches when trying to playing slow shots or find themselves 'push shotting' the ball, while Eric Bristow who coined the phrase 'dartitis' either couldn't release the dart at all, or would get the trajectory all wrong and have the poor caller hopping around like Michael Flatley in Riverdance, after discharging his 'arrers' towards the poor bloke's toes.

The yips happen to many sportsmen, and for no reason. Let's hope – with the breakthroughs in modern medical science – that this disease and terrible affliction can be overcome in the near future.

Some people have careers that depend on it.

31
THE UNLUCKIEST DISMISSAL EVER

A few years ago I used to open the batting with a hard-hitting Australian by the name of Brett Irwin. Brett was playing one day at Watford Town and pushed a forward defensive shot with the ball going out to the covers. Unfortunately his bat broke in the process, and a piece of the bat went backwards onto his stumps dislodging the bails. Brett was given out hit wicket.

32
THE DRINKS BREAK

It is very rare that The Middle Stump discusses a non-alcoholic beverage, but there seems to be a trend in club cricket at present which is both alarming and distressing. It is the poor quality of drinks break occurring throughout the game, and it needs to be sorted. It's an integral part of an afternoon's cricket and one that we all look forward to on a summer's day, having spent twenty-odd overs in the field. So I'm beginning the campaign to bring back a proper drinks break right here and now.

The drinks break is a funny old concept. First of all, you drink out of plastic cups that probably haven't been washed up. You'll use these several times on a hot summer's day, when each side gets two breaks per innings. You will have made a mental note of the festering cold sore on the lip of their overseas Australian quick bowler getting larger throughout the day, yet you still end up potentially using the same drinking vessel as him. None of your team mates bothers to wash up the cups and they are just reused an hour or so later. All manner of bacteria and diseases will be multiplying around the rim. The rim of the cups that is, and not just of the cusp of the Aussie's mouth. You wouldn't use his knife and fork at tea for your salad, yet drink out of the same beaker. No to coleslaw, but yes to cold sore.

I don't know about where you play your cricket, but in the Saracens Hertfordshire Cricket League we have a directive that the opposition are not charged more than £40 for their tea. This arose from some clubs a few years back taking the piss and charging through the roof for a couple of bits of stale bread with a slab of cheese stuck in the middle. Occasionally, if you went to a posh club like Harpenden, you got stuff like king prawns, but tucking into that was about as rare as the merits of your overseas Australian debating the feud between the Montagues and the Capulets in *Romeo and Juliet*. In general though, the quality of tea, and of orange squash in the drinks break was of a decent standard.

The price has been stuck at £40 per team for a number of years, and with the rising price of food in general affecting world markets, and therefore the index-linked cricket tea, the one place that clubs can scrimp and save a few pennies is on the orange squash. Having to feed 22 players, an umpire and two scorers for £80 isn't easy in these post-Brexit times.

My club is no different. A fortieth of Asda own-brand orange or Kia Ora is not ideal having been out in the field for an hour and a half (after twelve Guinnesses the previous night). When you have a throat as dry as Gandhi's flip-flop you need something that will hit the spot. While Kia Ora ran an advert back in the 1980s with the slogan, 'It's too orangey for crows, it's just for me and my dog' – it ain't too orangey for me and my team mates, I can tell you!

At the other end of the drinks break spectrum you used to get some clubs who made it too strong. This was no good either and made you end up with a similar feeling as if you had just rubbed your larynx into a nettle bush. You know what I mean? Similar to Elton John before he had the operation on his throat, but this is more Candle in the Windpipe if you get my drift?

The days of lime cordial for cricketers seem to be a thing of the past. I haven't seen a jug of lime cordial for donkey's years, although it used to be a regular occurrence. Posh, rich clubs would have a bit of dandelion and burdock (OK, lashings of ginger beer might be taking it too far), but that has gone out of the window, too.

What clubs need is a bit of double concentrate orange squash, and offer an alternative choice of blackcurrant. Lime is good, while a hot toddy on a cold day goes down a treat. Even water can be refreshing, but one thing is a must ... it needs to go in the fridge.

Some players use the drinks break for different things. The skipper usually wants a team talk, the bowler generally wants a rest, someone will spark up a fag, someone will go for a pee, others for a number two and there is always one who uses it as an excuse to chat up some decent-looking Doris on the boundary. Whatever you use it for, it is a beautiful thing; an oasis of 5 minutes' calm and of not having to chase leather around a dusty old pitch. The drinks break is sacred and shouldn't be messed with. It is an integral part of the game and one which should be revered. Yorkshire Tea ran a Cricket Tea Challenge a while back, so maybe some innovative squash manufacturer could do something similar for the drinks break?

So, with the quality of the drinks break declining at an alarming rate, we make a call to all cricket clubs – keep it at a decent strength, keep it real. Bring back the proper drinks break!

33
CRICKET THIEVES

Very, very occasionally you will play club cricket and find that you have had your dressing room turned over. It is a sad thing and nothing causes more anger than this, it's worse than tamely chipping one to cover when you're the last wicket and there are just four runs to win. It certainly takes the gloss off a win – put it that way.

As the writer of this book I pride myself on being a club cricketer writing about cricket. However, I am sure that all of you who have played club cricket are aware that there is a certain type of low-life who preys not just on cricket clubs, but on all sports clubs. These are the guys who, when you are out there in the heat of battle, go into your changing room and nick whatever they can. These people are the lowest of the low and all of the cricket family should be aware of such individuals.

The reasoning behind my case was seeing a post on Twitter recently from a certain cricket club up on the Lancashire coast. They got turned over recently and it seems the gentleman responsible has been targeting cricket and rugby clubs across the country. Clubs throughout the UK have all been done over by these bastards and they need catching – pronto. Often these blokes (for they are nearly always men), have conversations with the players and is even knowledgeable about the local clubs and cricket within the area. He then goes and nicks whatever he can lay his filthy little mitts on, before disappearing into the distance.

Con men can be like this. A few years back one chap in Surrey went to a few clubs and even helped out doing the washing-up after the tea interval before driving some poor sod's automobile out of the car park. Another chap back in the 1980s went to a cricket club befriending the players, before borrowing money from his new-found friends for a family emergency and did a Lord Lucan. They weren't the first ones to experience this man's modus operandi.

We had a chap in North London cricket a few years ago who turned over three cricket clubs in a day and was caught with a decent sum of cash on him, as this happened in the days before debit cards were commonplace.

Cricket clubs are prone to this. When it's 30°C and you've run off the beer and curry from the night before, the smell of a cricket changing room can be extraordinarily pungent (to say the least), meaning that the windows are generally left open. This is an open invitation to the dressing room thief, even when the door is locked. Air conditioning doesn't seem to have caught on in most of the grounds that I play at.

A few years ago we had a spate of thieves preying on our ground, and the boys were pretty desperate to catch one in the act. After the opposition had been done three times in one season we decided to take matters into our own hands. We made a pact that if we should catch someone red-handed, the whole team would perform some Michael Flatley-esque dancing on him in cricket spikes before turning the individual over to the police. The New Zealand pack of the 1990s, when they caught a forward lying on the wrong side and trying to slow the ball down, would have had nothing on us if we had got going. Fortunately for the thief, he didn't return.

Ex-England bowling coach Kevin Shine had the same idea a few years back when he caught a thief in the act at our ground during a Middlesex 2nd XI game. As it was a hot summer's day, the individual was only wearing a pair of shorts, and Shine dragged him by the hair over the gravel in the car park before handing him over to the police. Fair play.

The advice from the police is to get all of your valuables together and lock them away somewhere safe, such as behind the bar. Do not, as one club did, collect all of the goodies and leave the 'vallies bag' on the dressing room floor to save the thief the aggravation of having to go through all of your pockets individually. I should also imagine that the plod don't recommend taking matters into your own hands either. So, cricket clubs, please be aware of this vermin that preys on our game.

34
THE TEA LADY

The people who prepare your tea are a godsend in every cricket club. They are wonderful human beings, who spend their Saturday afternoon trying not to get burned on the urn. To these people The Ashes in cricket are the crispy skin of their wrists as they brush against yet another boiling pot.

They come in many shapes, ages, sizes and genders, yet for some reason they are always known as the tea lady. They range from an 89-year-old woman who does them at our club to a rather stressed out 15-year-old who sorts out catering for three separate XIs at another local club I know. They can be bored, apathetic adolescents who have no interest in the game, or elderly women who rule their clubhouse and the chaps with a fist of iron. Steadfast and adorned in their uniform of a pinny, one glare from this woman and players who have been full of dissent to all and sundry out on the pitch suddenly turn into the meekest of lambs.

An integral part of her duty is to warn off anyone attempting to eat the tea before the players get to fill their boots. Or more to the point, their stomachs. Cricket club dogs, watchers, players and kids will all try to nick a sandwich or a bit of cake before tea time comes around, so this woman has to have eyes in the back of her head.

Some clubs aren't lucky enough to have a tea lady. With this being the case, the players have to do the honours, taking it in turn to feed the masses in whites. This can lead to some interesting teas and the skipper only having ten men on the pitch after 4.30pm. You'll see these individuals walking around supermarkets on Friday nights or Saturday mornings putting far more thought and effort into their team mates' cricket tea than they would for their own weekly shop, their trolley normally being full to the brim with microwave meals for one. Sometimes entrusting a player to do teas can go drastically wrong. One gentleman at my club was spotted putting tea bags directly into the boiling water urn.

The tea lady has changed over the years. Today's health and safety regulations (I am pleased to say) mean that the ones who used to make the tea with a cigarette hanging out of their mouths – leaving half of a Rothmans in your Ploughman's – are a thing of the past.

In the professional game, nowhere epitomises the tea lady more than in the Ladies' Pavilion at Worcester. Dressed in pinnies, these wonderful women sell off slices of an array of cakes at a quid a slice and many a journalist looks forward to his visit to the banks of the River Severn just to take advantage of the lemon cake. Worcestershire player Jack Shantry once told me that his father can regularly be found on the steps of the Ladies' Pavilion covered in crumbs.

These people are just as important in any cricket club as the players or the groundsman. They need looking after and you should always be polite to them, whether it's in your own pavilion or in the opposition's. Always take your plate back to them and thank them for a wonderful tea, even if it tasted like gruel. They deserve gratitude.

35
RIVALS

Whatever club you play for, there will always be a grudge match at some point in the season. There's sure to be a side that your team mates hate and you'll even see them beginning to take things rather more seriously for this game. Some might even forego the obligatory ten pints on a Friday night as they prepare for battle. This is the one that they want to win more than any other over a season.

There can be a variety of reasons behind this. Historical rivalry, a local derby or a previous encounter full of downright cheating can all play their part in why it's such a big game. You will hear stories about this club all season and you may even hear the odd song being sung about them as well, should you have a talented lyricist among your ranks.

There's always a character in the opposition side that you love to hate, too. This man will be a *bête noire* who will play up according to the fixture. I have known of two skippers who were the *bêtes noire* of their respective sides and actually even refused to shake hands prior to the toss.

Rivalry like this regularly crops up owing to cheating during the previous season. An umpire who gives their star man not out despite him edging the ball to second slip can rankle somewhat among the boys and it breeds animosity. When this bloke follows it up by 'gunning' four of your own lads lbw, you want revenge and will bide your time to wreak your own terrible havoc. It is not unknown for clubbies to get their own back four or five years later.

There'll be members of your own side who'll moan about everything at this rival club. They'll describe the opposition as weirdos, complain about everything from the size of your changing room to the tea to the wrong lager behind the bar. Nothing is good enough and they'll continually look to pick holes in the opposition on and off the pitch. In turn, this is taught to the team youngsters who when they reach their 30s or 40s are likewise embittered enough to then pass down their 'knowledge' to their children. And so it goes on. In turn, the *bête noire* of the opposition has his own offspring and they pick up family traits which cause friction with your own kids. Some of these rivalries are passed down from generation to generation and have been running for 60 or 70 years.

The movement of players from club to club, which is becoming more common in the modern age, is another reason why games can have that little bit of extra added spice attached to them. The poaching of players is becoming more usual at club level and particularly when there is money involved, this can add fuel to the fire. If you have spent a lifetime coaching a child since he was 5 years old, only for him to depart to pastures new for a £100 a game, expect the volume button to be turned up in one of these fixtures.

There are also some clubs who hate everyone and everyone hates them. At the other end of the spectrum, there are some local rivals who get on well and all should be forgotten about over a post-match pint. Sometimes it has been known to go over the top. A photograph on Twitter showed an Australian club that were neck and neck with their rivals in the league, going into the final game of the season. They turned up on the Saturday only to find that their square had been dug up and what looked like a pick axe had been used to decimate the wicket. The damage had gone in at least a couple of feet deep. It didn't take a rocket scientist to work out who had done such a deed.

It doesn't matter if you are new to a side or if you have played for your club for 30 years – one of your contractual obligations is that you are expected to hate this rival club. I have seen many Australians get involved in the on-pitch banter despite them only having been at their club for a matter of weeks. This is learned behaviour, ingrained into them from experienced clubbies.

No matter what happens and no matter the level of animosity between you and this club, this is one game that you will want to play in … and win at any cost.

36
THE PARK PITCH

At some point in your club career you will play cricket on a park pitch. It may even be your home ground. It's a ground prepared and 'cared for' by a council groundsman who is just about capable of painting white lines on a crease. This man is not renowned for the loving care that he puts into a wicket and often the results show. A Friday night out in one of our city centres is not as dangerous as playing on a park pitch.

If you play at a decent standard then the chances of playing at such a venue is reduced. The better clubs have private grounds, but still they will come across a park pitch. Even the professionals have to cope with it as Middlesex opening bowler Tim Murtagh once discovered. Playing Oxford University at The Parks, a young couple suddenly walked aimlessly across the pitch. Though told to get off by players, umpires and a sparse crowd they were in a world of their own. Murtagh then offered the young chap a chance to bowl and he ran in before throwing –something that would have resulted in a serious examination of his action from the ICC – a horrendous wide down towards third slip. Murtagh got the ball back from him and everyone went on their merry way. It was a surreal moment in the professional game.

A park pitch can be dangerous. They play better when wet than in midsummer when they aren't watered. This the time of year that they then crack up and get naughty. Other dangers associated with the park pitch can be junkies' discarded heroin needles, dog turds and broken bottles for unwitting fielders to negotiate their way around. Sharp shards of the necks of Budweiser bottles are scattered around many a local park.

Rarely do park pitches have sightscreens as these are like a moth to a flame for local kids with vandal tendencies. I know of one club who even bring the stumps in at the tea interval so that the local 'yoof' don't nick them. One ground I know of in Dagenham even has a white tower block acting as a natural sightscreen just behind the bowler's arm – at least they can't try to scarper with that while you're eating your cheese and pickle sarnies....

Because of all these things, the phrase 'That's park' has come into the cricketing vocabulary. If someone does something stupid his team mates would often say 'Oh, that's village.' In my neck of the woods, suburban North London, it is always referred to as being 'park'.

Park cricket goes on all over the UK. It's awash with cricketers playing in black trainers or back in the 1980s an England or Spurs shirt. I got out to a 'park' bowler owing to the fact that the blue and red of his 1982 England World Cup kit bedazzled me and I was trudged off for with low score. My team mates serenaded me with the song of 'We are Ron's 22' all day afterwards. I have also known of an opening bat who was caught first ball of the game by a chap wearing Jesus sandals. Kiss me quick hats of the variety found at seaside resorts are also deemed 'park'.

The other thing about park cricket is that you have to go miles to fetch the ball when your bowler gets slapped for a boundary. There's no natural foliage to stop it in these places, the boundary is often a line painted in the middle of a huge space. I have seen many a clubbie having to fetch a ball from 200 yards past the boundary.

Park cricket is often full of interruptions as gangs of feral youths and packs of equally feral dogs regularly interrupt play. Park cricket can often finish at 8.30 at night in the pitch black, with some quick bowler steaming in at you on a cracked pitch.

At the other extreme I've seen games finished by 3.00pm as one side gets skittled out for a low score. A combination of a dodgy track and long grass, where full-blooded pulls will only get you a single, can often mean an early finish.

Changing rooms can often be a Portakabin as they have been burned down or deemed unsafe. Showers don't exist. We all started playing in a 3rd or lower XI and I personally have played on many parks. I am surprised that I haven't gone blind from all the canine excreta that I have dived into head first.

If I have painted a bleak picture then you'd better get used to it as a club cricketer.

37
OTHER THINGS DEEMED 'PARK' OR 'VILLAGE'

As well as black trainers, England football tops and kiss me quick hats mentioned in the previous chapter, here is a selection of other things that you'll see during your club career that are deemed 'park' or 'village'.

Turning up with a can of lager in your hand. For some reason this is deemed unacceptable at club cricket level, yet it is perfectly acceptable to pop open a bottle of champers or to crack on with a cheeky gin and tonic at Lord's at 11 o'clock in the morning.

Any type of hat that isn't a cricket hat – kiss me quick hats, baseball caps, panamas or international cricket sun hats. Park cricketers also sport a variety of colours and not the uniform hat/cap which is the official headwear for your club.

Batsmen coming out with no gloves.

Long socks – of any colour except white – being pulled up behind the pads to knee-level.

White canvas trainers. From the days of Dunlop Green Flash to Converse All Star combat trainers, these have been responsible for many a broken metatarsal.

Appealing for lbws from fine leg or square leg.

Appealing for stumpings or run-outs at the striker's end from mid-off or mid-on.

Hitting a full toss directly up in the air to cover.

Shell suit trousers. In addition to that, you can throw white chinos into the mix, or even white jeans – like the ones that the woman in the Bodyform advert used to run down the beach in as she was allegedly in full flow. Yeah, them.

Right-arm around the wicket opening bowlers to right-handers.

Batsmen not taking any kind of guard.

Batsmen taking an off-stump guard.

Wicketkeepers standing back to spinners... In fact not even standing back but standing on the edge of the cut strip approximately 2 yards behind the stumps in no man's land.

Said wicketkeeper throwing the ball at the stumps every delivery in the vain hope of getting a stumping.

Tucking trousers into socks.

Any white football top. As mentioned earlier these are often England and Spurs shirts. Bolton Wanderers, MK Dons, Swansea City, Fulham or even Real Madrid shirts are totally unacceptable attire in which to play cricket. Especially those with bloody 'Ronaldo' written on the back. England rugby shirts also fall into the same category with double park points for any kit with a sponsor's name on the front.

The use of nicknames in the scorebook.

The use of Christian names in the scorebook.

Drawing a duck in when a player has scored nought in the scorebook.

Writing the words 'Quack quack' in the batting column of a player who has scored nought in the scorebook.

T20 coloured clothing, unless of course you are playing a game of T20 that requires coloured clothing.

Not having a scoreboard and having to shout the score out to those in the middle.

£3.99 cricket balls from cheap bargain sports warehouses that break bats, fingers and have a lacquer on them that chips off after three overs. Despite this the balls retain their hardness for a good 600–700 overs and are harder than Bruce Lee, Muhammad Ali and those gobstoppers that we bought as kids in the 1970s.

Eating a pre-prepared tea that has been sitting in the sun for three hours on the edge of the boundary.

Not turning up with bails, stumps, balls, etc.

Coming out to bat with a thigh pad on the outside of your kit.

Playing in shorts. Training in shorts is, however, totally acceptable. Playing in shorts is not.

The swapping of kit between incoming and outgoing batsmen. Bats and helmets do get exchanged from time to time, but pads and a box? A massive no-no.

Astroturf pitches which can result in four byes over the keeper's head being top run scorer.

White shirts, long-sleeve school shirts. Fine for business attire but not on a cricket pitch please, gents.

Turning up in your whites 5 minutes before the game is due to start. Leaving in your whites is also park. Leaving before the end of a game is a criminal offence.

Smoking on the pitch.

Turning up with your kit in a supermarket carrier bag.

A cricket shirt with the name of your favourite international player on the back of it.

Taking a mobile phone onto a cricket pitch. Double points for players using it while fielding down at fine leg. Triple points for being in the middle of a text and allowing a ball to go for four runs.

Not being padded up when you are the next man in. Even more so if you have started to take off your pads with two balls left in a fit of pique at not getting a bat, only for a wicket to fall on the penultimate ball.

All 22 players going off home straight after the game without having a beer. Some clubs don't have a clubhouse for a variety of reasons but should then choose a local hostelry for their after-match pint. They should invite the opposition to join them. Going home straight after the game is totally 'park'.

38
THE BENT UMPIRE

There's one of these in every far-flung corner of the cricketing world. They are there to ruin the Saturdays of you and I, even more so than when you get rained off and end up having to go shopping at Lakeside or Westfield with the Mrs. These people are a curse on the game, and exist in every league in Britain. They have gunned more people than a sniper, made more people walk than an Italian car manufacturer, lifted more than a steroid-filled body builder and raised more fingers than your average gynaecologist ... ladies and gents, I bring you the curse of the bent umpire.

Now, before I start, there is a vast difference between the bent umpire and the incompetent fool who has the misfortune to be stuck out there so his team don't get docked points. The two can often be confused, but one is an outright cheating bastard, while the other is just clueless. There is a chap who umpires in the lower reaches of the Hertfordshire League who has triggered eight of our batsmen lbw in the past two seasons. I do not think this bloke is a cheat, I just think he is excitable, shows a lack of careful judgement when it comes to balls pitching outside leg stump and tends to give for both sides. He is what is known in the trade as a giver, although many of the middle-order batsmen in our club would prefer he was a receiver. Of their right fist.

The bent umpire, on the other hand is the out and out cheat who deliberately gives decisions for his side and is about as welcome in club cricket as a wet fart in borrowed whites. He has many ways of giving his side the advantage and woe betide the overseas player's sorry little Australian arse should he play a beautiful cover drive all along the carpet for four runs early in his knock, as this gentleman will need no excuse to gun him after that. Should the ball hit his pads, he is 'Mark Knopfler' – in dire straits.

The overseas player is the staple diet of the bent umpire, and while the opposition captain is occasionally given the benefit of the doubt (due to him having to adjudicate the said adjudicator), the overseas is cannon fodder. Often jovial and your best mate at the start of play, the rapport between you and the said chap tends to wear thin after a while, and by the end of play it's more like relations between Israel and Palestine (given that by now he has sent half your side back to the hutch). He loves to be in the game – the absolute centre of attention. All the best umpires go unnoticed.

I would guess that many of these people have boring desk jobs, where they are shouted at on a regular basis and have often been bullied. Saturday afternoon is their chance for revenge, their bit of power and their way of leaving a legacy. They may be qualified or not, it matters not one jot. Many of the worst of this breed sport the word 'Nompere' on their tie, or have ACO official badges on their coats. Throughout the course of the season, most of them will secure more points for their side than the bloke who is named player of the year at the club dinner.

This man (for I have never seen a cheating female umpire) has a number of other tricks up his sleeve. When his team is batting first, he'll to give one or two of his own tail-enders out lbw or caught behind, to 'prove' that he isn't a cheat. These are known as his sacrificial lambs, and you can bet your bollocks to a barn dance that in return, three of your top four will be seeing him lift a digit after the tea interval. He will then no doubt say in the bar, 'I give for both sides' or other such rubbish. I have even known of a captain that would decide whether to bat or bowl first, based on the reputation of the opposition umpire.

Another of his tricks is to unsettle your bowler. No-balling a guy who hasn't stepped over the line all season is a great way of putting the odd doubt into a bowler's head. These gentlemen normally base their out/not out decision on the volume of the appeal, and doesn't his opening bowler know it? In fact, the bowler often fields at square leg when he isn't bowling, so he can share a joke with the bloke who has just ruined your week.

The caught behind is another favourite, his hearing going from Beethoven's to that of a bat depending on which team is at the crease. He treats stumpings in a similar way. When your lads are batting his eyesight will be hawk-like, but when his team take to the crease it'll be more like David Blunkett's.

Rain brings this man into his element. He'll be keen on a return to the action if his team looks like winning, but if his side is looking like losing, you won't get this man out on the pitch for love nor money. He will slam the door shut on the game quicker than if a Jehovah's Witness had knocked on his.

I am yet to hear of the bent umpire who has done anyone for handling the ball, hitting the ball twice or timed out, but I am sure these situations must have occurred around the country. Middle Stump blogger Thorpster was, however, given out obstructing the field a few years back, when he and a bowler collided mid-pitch with the ball in the air. You guessed it – it was their umpire, not ours!

I was told a magnificent story by a club down in South Wales a few years ago. They had an umpire who was bent and they knew when a no-ball was coming. Allegedly, say for instance the third ball of every other over would be called a no-ball, no matter where the bowler's feet landed. This, in effect, allowed the batsman a free hit and he could slog at will, knowing that he wasn't going to get out. It does make you wonder doesn't it?

The bent umpire has many differing ways of dispatching his prey. A quick draw is often preferred, but some like the slow kill á la Rudi Koertzen. Like a cat with a mouse, they prefer to have their kill drawn out. Billy Bowden crooked fingers occur these days, too, although the Australian style of the raised arm directly above the head seems to be not so much de rigueur among club cricketers.

Even worse are these characters who almost give the batsman a heart attack when they raise their finger simply to point down the leg side to indicate a not out. Batsmen are twitchy enough as it is without these individuals bringing their arm around their waist only to point down the leg side. It is the cricketing equivalent of walking away from the hangman's noose.

Finally, just when you think this man's work is done, and the game is meandering towards a draw, the umpire strikes back. Like Darth Vader, this man shows the number eleven his dark side as he looks for any excuse to finish the game off and get back in the hutch for his post-match pint. This can be the fate of both numbers ten and eleven, depending on how cold a day it is or whether he has a drink problem.

These people are the fabric of our game, and no matter how much we moan about them – and trust me, I have for nearly 30 years – they're still out there.

Have a good weekend everyone. And for fuck's sake, use your bat, not your pads!

39
THE DEATH OF SUNDAY CRICKET

Cricket is changing in the UK almost from one season to the next. As a clubbie you may find that you make yourself available for a game of Sunday cricket and that you have to cancel the fixture. Or the opposition does. Here's my take on the demise of the Sunday game.

I don't know about you, but in my opinion, and most definitely in the south-east, there is something facing extinction. The World Wildlife Fund might go on about elephants, tigers or even pandas, although the only thing in England to be found in the undergrowth that eats, shoots and leaves is the odd clubbie after a team visit to a nightclub. For bonding purposes of course. One thing that is dying on its arse though is Sunday cricket, and that is a very sad thing for club cricketers across the land.

Thirty years ago, Sunday cricket at my club in North London was stronger than Saturday cricket. We would regularly put three teams out on a Sunday, compared to two on a Saturday. Even 20 years ago, we would play sides from the Premier Division in Hertfordshire, Middlesex or Essex on a home and away basis. For the uninitiated, this means that your first team play each other, say for instance on your ground, while the second string play each other on their ground. This tended to work very well, apart from one instance in the 1980s when a fixture cock-up meant that our weak Sunday 2nd XI faced a strong Ilford 1st team featuring Essex's Alan Lilley who needed to play himself back into form after an injury. Ilford amassed a mere 380, as Lilley helped himself to a very quick 190. Our lads would have preferred to bowl to Lily Allen than Alan Lilley.

It wasn't always like this though, and Sunday cricket was strong. It was also sociable with sides having a beer afterwards, always buying a jug for the oppo, as well as being good cricket. It was an opportunity to play against sides that had been promoted or relegated from your league, and against people that you knew, often on stunning, picturesque grounds that you didn't have the opportunity to play on in the league on a Saturday. You would play against wandering teams (teams with no home ground) with magnificent names like the Malcontents or Jackdaws. The day would no doubt be finished off with six or seven of you in a curry house at midnight.

Now I look at Sunday cricket and feel pity for the youngsters. Good cricket clubs, sides who play Premier League cricket cannot fulfil their Sunday fixtures. I look at sides that I know who have won the National Cup at Lord's who can't manage to put a side out on a Sunday.

So why is this? Sunday shopping hours have made a difference. Many a cricketer who would have played back in the day, now finds himself with that glazed look upon him as he is dragged around some faceless shopping mall on the sabbath. There's also other stuff to do these days, too. For one thing, pubs are open longer. Until the early 1990s they opened from 12 noon until 2.30pm on a Sunday afternoon and then could open from 7.00pm until 10.30pm. Now they stay open all day. I'm not saying all cricketers are pissheads (although many I know are) but family commitments such as meals in the pub in the afternoon seem to have taken precedence. Boozers have also become more family orientated and a place to take the kids, as opposed to the spit and sawdust of yesteryear. It's not like many of my team mates have suddenly found Jesus, it has to be said!

Sunday cricket has just grown weaker and weaker over the years. It doesn't help that many of the sides who play Sunday cricket now won't come up to your bar for religious or cultural reasons, thus meaning that the home team are less inclined to stay. If there are opposition in your bar, the onus is on the home team to hang around and show them hospitality. Our own club has tried using Sunday cricket as a development side, but when you get a fixture through the

Conference and a side comes along professing to be weak or medium/weak, proceeds to rattle up 400 in 40 overs against a few teenagers and then rings the boundary with four outriders from the first ball of the second innings, you really wonder if it's all worthwhile?

I am a great believer in time games as opposed to limited overs, with 20 overs commencing at 6.30pm. This teaches a good skipper how to dangle the carrot and winkle a side out by utilising his slow bowlers in tandem with close catchers. There is a place still for the draw in the game in my opinion.

I don't really fully understand why Sunday cricket is dying out, though. You see sides on Saturday run five or six XIs, but can't get a side out on a Sunday. Surely if you're making yourself available to play in the Saturday 4th or 5th XI for these clubs, and playing on park or school grounds, you'd rather play on picturesque club grounds on a Sunday?
We did try to join a league a few years back but the travel and lethargy by our own lads to go some distance for a decent game took its toll. Initiatives such as development XIs, or sides playing 20-over bashes on a Sunday are now starting to take shape, as something as had to be done. It really had to happen – without it, the game that you and I love would have suffered greatly at grass roots level. I hope and pray, for the sake of clubs across the land, that it works.

40
BRICKING IT

All clubbies brick it from time to time. In fact all cricketers do, even at a professional level. There'll come a time in your career when you find out that adrenalin is brown and lumpy. There are various ways in which you will brick it – how you deal with it will define how good a player you are. At least half of cricket is played in the head and adrenalin does funny things to people. It is why cricket is such a wonderful game.

The most obvious way of bricking it is a batsman facing a quick bowler. Never mind short leg, you often will see them dancing on square leg's toes. When it gets hostile out in the middle, the last place you want to be going is backwards. It's not just out in the middle, either. You should see the state of some clubbies before they go into bat.

Some go quiet, while some get loud. Some smoke 20 cigarettes and some are known to pace the boundary for four or five laps. At this point some smart arse who is out early tells the waiting batsmen that the bowling is quick – which, let's face it, is about as much use as Ann Frank's drum kit. You want your top order to be full of bravado, even if the bowler is quick. Phrases like 'You can play him with your cock, mate' are what your batters need to be hearing.

There are other ways of bricking it, though. A deliberate beamer from a bowler is bricking it in my eyes. It's cowardly. For bowlers there is a different sort of pressure, especially towards the end of an innings. Getting the ball in the right place can be a tough job when the pressure is on and your accuracy (or lack of it) can win or lose the game. Any bowler who puts his hand up to do the job in the first place does not brick it in my book. Win or lose.

Then there's the batsman who blocks out for a draw instead of going for the win. My Australian chums would describe this bloke as a 'pea heart'. I have seen too many games of club cricket ruined by people going for a draw and being too scared to lose.

Consider, too, the average-obsessed clubbie who has a look at the league fixtures. If you are playing the top of the league side with a quick bowler in their ranks you may find him unavailable due to a 'wedding' or having to go to his 'kids' school summer fête'. Yeah right.

Then you have the captain. The captain has a responsibility to make a decent game of cricket. Good captains keep their spinners on as long as possible if they are taking wickets and pack men around the bat. Skippers who brick it put men on the fence at the first sign of a boundary and you often see them following the ball. They are responsible for draws in league cricket as much as the captain who tells his side to block it out when they are only four wickets down.

Fielders brick it, too. A late dive often saves you from running to the boundary which means that your team mate has to get it. The other way of bricking it is diving over the ball so that you don't get hurt. I have seen many fielders take the ball on the bounce instead of running in and going for the catch. I would rather the ball went for four and my player actually went for it. Sticking out a hand gingerly as someone creams one along the ground at you too, is known as bricking it and often results in broken fingers. If you go at the ball properly it can smart a little but it is better than getting one on the tip of the finger.

Umpires are not immune from bricking it. I have seen many not want to give the last man out lbw in case it all kicks off. Likewise, I have seen plumb lbw shouts first ball of the game not given as it is too early for the umpire to give it.

So, in club cricket there will be a time when you might brick it. It is not down to ability or technique but just pure heart. It is how you deal with the pressure and 'how much ticker you have' as the Australians say that will define you as a good team man by your fellow clubbies. The spilling of a bit of blood always establishes your place in a side.

Come on, guys – try not to brick it! To quote Kipling (Rudyard and not 'Mr' who provides those wonderful cakes for your cricket tea), 'And – which is more – you'll be a man, my son!'

41
THE NUMBERS IN CLUB CRICKET

The figures of people playing club cricket are declining. There are many reasons why, but I have tried to cover a few of them in the piece below. Despite having 15,000 clubs in the UK and 900,000 players of recreational standard, the players figure was up to over a million a few years ago.

Last year the ECB produced alarming figures regarding the drop in the amount of people playing cricket at club level. Grass roots cricket is taking a hiding, so they say. The amount of people donning the whites for their local club has gone down quicker than the value of sterling in these post-Brexit times. Surely it's time that we did something about it? Sport in general has become all about money as opposed to pure competition, and it has to stop.

I'm not here to say I told you so, but regular readers of my blog, The Middle Stump, will know that we have been bemoaning this fact for a number of years. It has suddenly become newsworthy now that the figures have been produced, but if you ask most of our readership, then we all knew a few years ago. The ECB are about as in touch with the cricketing public in the UK as George Osborne is with the working class.

Until cricket is shown on free-to-air TV, the figures will always be the same. The international game has been sold off to Sky on TV, which only attracts the kids whose parents can afford it. The yoof don't grow up with the names any more, and they have lost the connection. My generation grew up on endless days of the summer game being on during the school holidays. It grew up on televised county cricket such as Gillette/NatWest or a Benson & Hedges Cup ties. We knew all the names, they were ours. They belonged to the people, or so we thought. Even if they didn't, we believed that they were our lads. We loved the avuncular Richie Benaud, the sheen on Peter West's bonce and the gravelly tones of John Arlott.

This was shown in the amount of kids who came to cricket out of inner-city London back in the 1980s and played county cricket. In my locality Keith Piper and Mark Alleyne came through the Haringey Cricket College, but then Graham Rose, Kevan James, Mike Gatting, John Emburey, Chris Lewis, Phil DeFreitas and many more came through schools in London. Who has come through recently via this route? Ravi Bopara and Billy Godleman are the only ones who spring to mind in the last ten years. While the initiatives of Chance to Shine and the like are great, counties could do a lot more with their players and links with schools, now that they are on 12-month contracts. State schools have a responsibility and it is shocking how few actually play the game.

People say football is the same and in some ways I can see similarities. Ask the supporters of Manchester United or Arsenal whether putting money before success – as I believe both of their clubs have done in recent years – has been good for their team? Sport has become more about money than it has about the game itself. We have situations in football where finishing fourth in the league is more important than winning a competition like the FA Cup, all because of money. Sides are happy not to compete, but to come fourth. Success brings people into the game, and the numbers playing rugby after the 2003 World Cup was indicative of that. In the UK we hosted the Olympics in 2012 and the games were supposed to leave a legacy. The only legacy that I can see is that the Olympic Village has been turned into private accommodation with sky-high rents and that the stadium has been given on a cheap lease to a Premier League football club who are not exactly hard up in the first place.

The difference between football and cricket though is that the Beeb show *Match of the Day* on a Saturday and Sunday night. Cricket has nothing, apart from Test highlights on the least-watched major channel. Anyone remember the feel-good factor within the game after the last series on free-to-air TV? Cast your mind back to the 2005 Ashes. Michael Vaughan wrote a piece in the *Telegraph* about an FA Cup-style competition in cricket to get interest in the game. We have to try something as it cannot continue to wither and die at club level.

While the ECB have made a number of mistakes, there are other factors that have come into play. The Sunday opening hours of pubs, Sunday shopping hours and the increasing number of channels on TV all give people far more choice in their entertainment – if you can call being dragged around the shops by your Mrs, or watching the *Eastenders* omnibus entertainment. Therefore, cricket has to compete even harder. The empty seats at Test venues over the last few years at the non-London grounds tell a sad story, so ticketing pricing also needs a radical rethink. Surely more people in the ground at cheaper ticket prices – buying refreshments and merchandise – is better for the game? Surely grounds not charging a fiver a pint so that parents are put off taking their lads (or lasses) needs a rethink, too? Equipment prices going through the roof don't help either. As mentioned before, a top-of-the-range bat can cost anything up to £500 – 'ow much?! Does this help people to play the game? The manufacturers also have a responsibility to make cricket accessible.

The money from Sky has been great for the county game, don't get me wrong. However, we MUST get cricket back on the mainstream box. Offer a channel a deal for county cricket and show the 50-over competition. Give the game back to the public, and you will increase interest. The game being inaccessible to all children could well kill the sport for future generations and the powers that be have to find a way to beam the game into more people's living rooms. The link between interest in the sport and playing the game is huge. How good would T20 be on a Friday night on Channel 4 for instance? The kids would fall in love with it. The IPL being shown on ITV4 in recent years has been hugely popular with the kids and not just those with Asian backgrounds

If the ECB have the attitude of 'let them eat cake', there might not be that many people at grass roots level to have a slice of it during the tea interval.

The game belongs to us all.

42
THE RUN OUT

'Yes ... No ... Yes ... Wait ... Oh shit, sorry.' How many times have you said those words while batting? How many times have you HEARD those words while batting?

No doubt hundreds, possibly thousands of you were run out last weekend all over the UK. If you're unlucky enough to be in with a batting partner who has communication impairment, you'll likely be left stranded, and he'll be about as popular with you as a rattlesnake in a lucky dip (to quote one well-known Australianism). It has happened for centuries, it will happen for centuries, and sometimes nothing is more amusing than the run out.

Seeing two blokes end up at the same end can result in the odd bit of disharmony among team mates. It can end up about as friendly as Paul McCartney and Heather Mills, especially if you have someone who can run like the aforementioned Ms Mills down at the other end. If that's the case, and you're someone who has the turning circle of an oil tanker (like my good self), the best thing to do is to lean on your bat and not budge, before you end up like the *Amoco Cadiz*, run aground in the English Channel. Your batting partners soon learn ... trust me. I'm speaking from personal experience.

A run out can cause big rows in the game. Confusion, chaos and antipathy reign regularly in these situations. Think of Ricky Ponting calling Duncan Fletcher a 'fucking cheat' as he hissed at the balcony on the way off, after Gary Pratt had thrown his stumps down in 2005. Anyone remember Mark Waugh versus India when Darren Lehmann took one for the team? The batsmen had crossed by the margin of a couple of centimetres, yet Lehmann walked.

By the same token, remember when Boycott was deliberately run out by Ian Botham in New Zealand in 1977? The was sliding away from

England due to the Yorkshireman's slow scoring, until, that is, Beefy called for a quick one and sent back Sir Geoffrey. Stranded mid-pitch, all Boycs could exclaim was, 'What have you done? What have you done?' Boycs also made himself about as popular as the Sheriff of Nottingham by running out local hero Derek Randall at Trent Bridge in 1977.

Some are just mental aberrations. Allan Donald in the 1999 World Cup semi-final, dropping his bat as the jubilant Australians whooped and hollered springs to mind.

However, nothing is more confusing than when a runner comes into play. Not even trying to work out Pythagoras' theorem after ten pints, the emotional state of my ex-wife or the ECB's public relations at present comes close to trying to watch a guy at square leg, two on the crease and the injured party not leaving his. Throw in stumps flying, people rowing and umpires' vision being blocked by the runner or a fielder, and you can see why it can get a tad bewildering. Then woe betide the runner who leaves his ground and gets the batsman he's supposedly running for, run out.

Nothing causes a decent rumble like a good 'Mankading'. Running out the chap backing up is the cricketing equivalent of the professional foul, or slyly moving your golf ball out of the rough when nobody's looking. Named after Vinoo Mankad who did it to Aussie player Bill Brown in 1948, the last well-known instance was Jos Buttler's dismissal by the Sri Lankan Senanayake a few years ago. Senna tablets when you're suffering from Delhi Belly would be preferable to the ramifications of this dismissal.

Obstructing a runner can get the juices flowing. Having to run around a bowler blocking someone on the turn can cause animosity. Remember how Sherwin Campbell getting blocked off in Barbados a few years back caused Steve Waugh to remove his side from the field under a hail of bottles? Middle Stump writer John Thorp was once given out in a league game as a leading edge sent the ball directly up in the air. As the bowler was about to complete a relatively simple caught and bowled, he found himself to taken out by The Middle Stump scribe's shoulder charge and he was promptly given out obstructing the field. Thorpster took his punishment well and went straight off with the umpire's words 'If you were playing hockey or rugger young man, you would be banned for six months' ringing in his ears!

Then you have the serial runners-out, and I don't mean fielding-wise, although Derek Randall would be in both camps. A brilliant cover fielder, he was a nightmare when batting and would regularly commit cricketing hara-kiri. Inzamam, Steve Waugh, Nasser Hussain, Geoff Boycott and Graeme Wood have seen off more partners than Henry VIII, Elizabeth Taylor and Jordan combined ... and I'm not talking about Chris. These people are the worst to bat with.

So why does it happen? Bad judgement? Bad communication? Too fast? Too slow? All of the above? Whatever happens there will be many more over the course of the summer.
The run out might be a waste of a wicket, the equivalent of a wasted vote or a criminal offence in some quarters, but one thing I do know ... they usually raise a laugh.

43
THE BOOZY CLUB CRICKET CURRY

Across the length and breadth of Britain from April to September, there is a common sight in every high street in the land. At around 10.30pm, possibly later, you will find cricketers having spent a day in the sun, replenished with lager in their clubhouse with just one thought on their mind ... where can I get a decent Ruby? As a man who has had three curries in one day before at cricket (when playing an Indian team we had saag aloo sarnies at tea and one of the oppo wives cooked one in their clubhouse after the game, before finally going for another one in a local restaurant at 11.00pm), I am someone experienced with regards to a cricketing curry.

Firstly, I am not condoning the behaviour that follows. I am just telling it like it is. And was. The local Indian restaurant is like a moth to a flame for cricketers. It's where teams bond and where you can finally laugh about that golden duck, that dropped catch or that over that went for 20. It's a place where your team mate finally forgives you for running him out or dropping that crucial catch off his bowling.

Every team has one of the following among their ranks:

The Organiser – this chap will be first in to ask for a table for ten. He will order for his team mates, knows the staff intimately and will have the nous and the know-how to be able to top up the table with cheaper veg dishes, thus keeping the cost down. This man knows that for every team mate, at least four popadoms need to be ordered. Experienced organisers keep the best dishes for themselves and plonk themselves next to the Youngster to hide the fact that their king prawn sizzling dish is hidden among the cheaper biryanis served to younger players. Often the captain, the organiser is the leader of the group. This man is skilled at sorting out bill disputes and leaving the restaurant so that you are all welcome back the following week, despite bad behaviour.

The Sleeper – one chap will generally fall asleep, and is often known to do a passable impression of Rip van Winkle, especially when the bill arrives. Depending on how many Cobras or Kingfishers this he's imbibed, he is known to fall asleep face-down in his curry leaving him as red-faced as Prince Harry after a week in Magaluf. I have seen many Sleepers miraculously wake up when the financial side of every curry is over.

The Miser – this chap, often the club treasurer, is tight and can compute within seconds to the exact penny, how much £85.39 is between seven of you. Alternatively if a bill comes to £52 between four of you and you all throw in £15 each, he will ask the waiter for change and dish out £2 each, not tipping the poor chap who has put up with all of your abuse, loud behaviour and loutishness for the last hour and a half. This gentleman is often known to complain about the bill, and will say that his stuff only came to £7, thus forcing his team mates to chip in extra. He'll probably even say he drank water while everyone else was on the lager.

The Other Miser – someone who will insist on ordering the most expensive dishes for himself and insisting that he pays the same as the youngster. He has similar traits to miser number one and the organiser in his choice of cuisine, but will not take the responsibility of the other two. Instead, having wolfed down his dish from the specials menu, he will often chip in the same amount as the poor bloke who has had a Madras and a boiled rice. Boiled rice is never on this man's menu, only the special fried. Like his miserly companions, he will drink more than his fair share of Kingfisher or Cobra but insist on paying the same amount as the Youngster who has had a Coke.

The Youngster – a junior member of the side, this chap will want to be seen out with the big boys. He'll probably order a biriyani, a korma, or, if he is feeling really adventurous, a chicken tikka masala. Generally keeps quiet sitting there laughing at the behaviour of his older, drunken team mates.

The Big Boy – this bloke will smash the popadoms into a thousand smithereens with his huge fist when they arrive. Often a quick bowler, he is known to order a vindaloo or a phall and winces with every mouthful despite his protestations that it's lovely. Will often eat the lime pickle straight when it arrives with the popadom and is known to drink the mint sauce dip. Three or four large bottles of Kingfisher will accompany this bloke's Ruby.

The Pig – this chap will over order, and eat everything on the table. If you are not quick enough, he will eat yours too, and has no concept of the shared experience curry house dining. Pigs can often be spotted behind a mountain of pilau rice and everyone else's food piled up high on his plate. This bloke will 'minesweep' whatever is left on the table when everyone is finished, too. Post curry, he can often be spotted after midnight wandering around our town centres with enough food to feed a small African country on the front of his T-shirt. Experienced Pigs will also wolf down the After Eights while his team mates are sorting out the bill.

The Bore – single, and with nothing better to do on a Saturday night, this bloke will talk you through his innings or his bowling spell in intimate detail just as you are trying to stop a Pig from taking your chicken dopiaza. This gentleman tends to be perched at the far reaches of the table as no one really wants to hear, for the fifth time, how he had a dubious lbw decision given against him.

The Prat – this bloke will be rude to the staff thinking he's amusing in front of his team mates. If not the staff, he will be rude to other customers in the restaurant and has been known to cause mass brawls as your visit coincides with the end-of-season meal of a local rugby club, before disappearing behind the shoulder of the Big Boy when it all kicks off. Waiters generally put up with the rude behaviour of this chap, due to the £100 or so they can make from their team mates late at night.

So wherever you play over a weekend, and no doubt many of you will go for a curry, try to be peaceful and be respectful to your local curry house owner.

44
GAMES THAT CLUBBIES PLAY

There will come a time in your club career that you are drawn into various games by bored team mates. Card games such as poker are the norm in most clubs but the enterprising clubbie will come up with something different. Many are played throughout the land due to a combination of rain delays, too much beer or general boredom. Here are a few of them…

One Hand, One Bounce – the standard fodder during rain breaks and often played indoors. Used by batting with a stump, the rule is that you can catch a team mate out should the ball only bounce once if you use one hand. Catches on the full are allowed with two. For health and safety reasons we implore that the law of defensive shots only is adhered to, as swinging a stump around in the confines of a dressing room can lead to all sorts of problems. Rumours abound that King Harold didn't lose an eye fighting against the Normans but was actually playing an early version of this game. However, I am not sure about Colin Milburn or the Nawab of Pataudi though. Again we advise that a tennis ball and not a cricket ball is used in this game unless you have a fondness for replacing lights and windows. Bored players of One Hand, One Bounce, for a laugh, often smash the ball around the changing room, although I have seen one chap do this and not only smash the light with the ball that he had hit but also left his stump impaled in the dressing room ceiling.

Boundary Bowls – getting out for a low score can leave three or four hours to kill and the most skilled operatives of this sport tend to be opening batsmen or opening bowlers who have the most time on their hands. The advent of boundary ropes in recent years at club level has reduced the number of clubbies you'll see playing such a pastime, as the traditional boundary flag made a great 'jack'. The rule of the game is to take a cricket ball around the boundary with you and get it nearest to the object that is deemed the jack. I have seen many an argument over who got nearest, especially when money is at stake.

The Water Slide – all you need for this one is three days of rain, some covers (ideally of the tarpaulin sheet variety and most definitely not roll-on roll-off covers), some washing-up liquid and team mates who are stupid enough to do it. It involves running up to the said sheet and diving head first along it. Whoever slides the furthest wins the game. Aficionados of this sport can manage to slide for over 22 yards.

Around the Stump – normally played after a few beers, this involves five of your team on one side and five on the other. You need a referee. The first runner sets off from each team to a waiting pint of beer. This needs to be downed in one. He (or she) then runs 20 yards further forward to a stump and you have to put your head down and run around the stump ten times before trying to get back relay-style to your second runner. The combination of beer and dizziness leads to some hilarious results, with players darting off in all sorts of directions, falling over and even taking out the opposition. It is advisable not to play this one the night before an important game as injuries are common.

Twat of the Match – in our club we used to have an award called 'Twat of the Match'. This was a team vote on who'd had the worst game during the day's play, although it was a kangaroo court at times. The recipient of Twat of the Match had to drink a half of lager, half of bitter, half of cider and a short of their choice within 2 minutes or whatever was left went down their pants. It might sound easy, but the volume and the gas tends to lead to projectile vomiting. After a golden duck and 0-40 I received this award at an away game where a wedding was taking place and, needing to visit the toilet urgently, I was forced to run through the reception, catching sick in my hands much to the chagrin of the bride's mother. The record time for downing the drinks, by the way, is 11 seconds.

The Sweepstake – can be used on a club visit to a professional game or on your return to your club should a game be going on there. Six or seven of you are required to put a pound into a pint pot. Every time a boundary is scored the pot passes on to the next person. Moving seats is not allowed except for toilet breaks and the said incumbent must return to the place where he was previously sitting. Whoever is left with the pot at the end of the game or innings, wins the money.

The Upside Down Pint – I visited a cricket club once where they had an Australian who, after the game, would do three pints on his head one after the other up against the dart board in their clubhouse. We then tried it at our club. You need the help of a willing couple of team mates to hold your legs up. You have to drink backwards and much of it can come back through your nose or spillages can go into your eyes. Set the stopwatch running for each competitor and the quickest to down the pint upside down, wins the game.

The Shut Your Eyes Game – quite possibly the most stupid game that I have ever heard of involved a few guys in our club. The game was meandering to a draw and our quick bowler was brought on. With three slips and a gulley, they decided to play a game in which you close your eyes when the ball is bowled. This can cause serious damage and not just a right-hander from your opening bowler as an easy catch hits you in the chest. Or even worse, in the face. There are no winners in this game.

The Bottle Game – now outlawed in our club on the grounds of health and safety. It involved keeping your feet behind a line and walking bottles on your hands as far as you could. You would then reach out and leave your bottle as far out as you could before getting back behind the line. The only rule in this is that your hands can't touch the ground (resulting in disqualification). Unfortunately one of our number exported this sport to Australia where the bottle collapsed going through the wrist of his new found Antipodean team mate. An urgent visit to the local A&E department was necessary and the sport has not been played since.

Speckles – a game played among squaddies, this has been known to have taken place in a cricket club in South Africa. If you want to find out what it is, Google it in the Urban Dictionary. It's more commonly known as 'Freckles'.

45
AN AMATEUR SPORT?

As a clubbie you will play against these people if you play at a decent enough standard. You probably won't be aware of the fact until they have smashed a double hundred very quickly or gone through your batting line-up quicker than a dose of salts. I originally wrote this article around four years ago and it then got worse. I then rewrote it a couple of years later … and the problem has worsened further…

Cricket on the village green, the local blacksmith belting the ball into the neighbouring village, playing against people who also held down similar professions and leaving work to play for fun. These are all a thing of the past. Money is now rife in club cricket and the game is poorer for it. The days of amateurism are well and truly over in club cricket now, yet the leagues which wish to remain amateur turn a blind eye.

The problem seems to have got worse with regard to the amounts now being bandied about in club cricket. One former professional confided in us that he was better off playing club cricket than he was when he was a professional. The cash he got from his Minor County, expenses and getting cash-in-hand from his club without paying tax on it meant that he was in a better financial position than when employed by a fairly large Test-staging county.

The ECB Premier Leagues fund clubs as part of their 'Raising the Standard' initiative, which was introduced in 1997. All clubs are supposed to have thriving junior sections to attain accreditation, but many prefer to throw this funding into the myopic view of putting a few quid into the pockets of players who will not be around in a few years. These players, in the main, show the loyalty of an alleyway tom cat, moving on to the next club who'll pay them a few more shekels. The money should surely be invested into junior sections. I am sure that this isn't where the money that is supposed to be filtered down to the 'grass roots' of the game is supposed to go.

It isn't just them. It is the equivalent of counties playing a host of Kolpak players, and this has filtered down the food chain with club cricket now.

Cricket tends to vary in terms of professionalism at club level across the country. In many leagues, a professional is allowed and critics argue that this has strengthened the standards. Many leagues in the south-east of England do not allow for payments to be made to any player, yet some clubs are blatantly flouting this. One ex-professional in a south-east league is allegedly on £500 a match in local cricket. Nice work if you can get it!

Other clubs have risen from non-entities to Premiership level in recent years, paying seven or eight players a week. A wage bill of nearly £1,000 a game is surely not good business practice for any organisation, and yet some of these clubs have extremely average junior sections. How the guys in lower XIs, who have paid their annual subs or match fees, feel about people in their own side who do exactly the same role, yet receive a brown envelope at the end of play, then God only knows! Clubs now prefer to 'tap up' promising youngsters from other local clubs, offering them inducements to play for them, rather than raising the standard of their own players. The amount of movement of players between clubs is now at its highest, and the days of cricketers having a club for life are becoming lesser with every season that passes

There is also the moral aspect, let alone those who expect a visit from those at Her Majesty's Revenue and Customs. Working all week, you want to challenge yourself – yes, you want to play cricket against like-minded individuals and if that person is better than you, then fair play. However, coming up against someone in division two or three of a league, who has recently been a professional or maybe a current pro in another part of the world just isn't cricket. Especially then said individual goes through your batting in seven or eight overs or smashes a ton very quickly, ruining the game for a lot of people. It isn't only in Premier League cricket where the remuneration is happening.

The problem has got worse and no doubt will continue to deteriorate. As the cash has flowed, behavioural standards in league cricket have got significantly worse. Journalist Steve James watched a club game recently and seemed astonished at the amount of 'chirp' and 'send-offs' on offer. I am sure this is a nationwide trend and I wonder if this is because of the financial incentives in club cricket? As umpires are turning a blind eye to bad behaviour on the pitch, league administrators are turning a blind eye to payments off the pitch. It doesn't take a rocket scientist to know that when an outfit suddenly gains a lot of players from Premier League clubs, or with Minor Counties experience, something dubious is going on. Proving it is a different matter.

Various guises, such as Director of Colts Cricket, come with a salary, and it just happens that the person in his newly founded – or perhaps newly funded – role plays on a Saturday in the league. Other ways around the issue are that the person is employed by an institution with links to the club.

As for the clubs, they are taking a short-termist view. The prize money on offer for winning leagues doesn't seem to match the wage bills. Clubs are making money through other revenue streams such as functions, weddings and the like, yet the money is not being ploughed back into grass roots and the junior sections. Even worse, grants are being given out in places with not all of the money finding its way towards the project it should have been for. That will come back to haunt some of these outfits in years to come.

Where or when will the buck, or bucks, stop? That is the defining question.

46

CRICKET NICKNAMES

Whatever country you play your cricket in, whether you go to a new club or not, or whatever level of the game you play, one thing is for certain: you *will* be given a nickname. Cricket is a sport where long periods of time are spent with your team mates, and many hours, many thoughts and many brain cells have been used up thinking of these nicknames. No matter how juvenile, how puerile or how crass, everyone who has donned the whites has one. Some are funny, some are clever, some are just awful and some have been downright genius. The cricketing nickname has been around since the year dot and will no doubt stay forever.

The public laughed a couple of years ago when Alastair Cook would refer to England players by sticking an '-y' on the end of their name. Straussy, Rooty, Belly, Broady, the only one he didn't do it to was Moeen Ali. However, some cricketing nicknames over the years have been far more thoughtful and amusing than this.

There have been the time-honoured ones such as if your name is Smith then you are Smudger, Miller would be Dusty, and those with the surname Hunt are often known as Isaac (work it out yourself). Others have been far more leftfield. Mark Waugh was known as Afghanistan (as in the Forgotten War) as he waited to make his debut when brother Steve, (aka Tugga) was an integral part of the Aussie side. Nicknames like Tugga are a play on the surname, others of this type including Andrew Strauss (Levi), John Crawley (Creepy) and Vic Marks (Skid). Allan Lamb was known as Legga but my favourite of this brand of nickname was ex-Gloucestershire player, Paul 'Human' Romaines.

Others have been more erudite plays on their surname. Worcestershire player Shaaiq Choudhry is known as Colin (after Colin Cowdrey), Tim Murtagh is known as Dial M (for Murtagh), you had Graham 'Picca' Dilley, while Chris Old was known as Chilly after going down in the scorebook as 'C. Old'. Allan Border was another of this ilk, being known as 'Herbie' after herbaceous border.

Other famous people give cricketers who share their surname their nickname. Jason 'Dizzy' Gillespie, Matty 'Herb' Elliott, or Steve 'Sid' James. Robert Russell, who took his nickname from a famous dog, is known so well by his nickname that many won't even know that I am talking about the ex-Gloucestershire and England keeper, Jack.

Sometimes nicknames can be longer and along the lines of those more familiar in boxing. Moeen Ali is known as 'The Beard that's Feared', Viv Richards was 'The Master Blaster' and Harbhajan Singh was the 'Turbanator'. A marketing man's dream, eh?

Sometimes it's your physical features that define such changing room wit. Ginger-haired Steve Kirby was known as 'Tango', while 'Two Metre Peter' Fulton and Joel 'Big Bird' Garner got their nicknames from their enormous height. David Gower was christened Lulu as his blond curls resembled those of the singer when he made his debut in 1978. Another to be rechristened after a Scottish female singer is Yorkshire quickie Jack Brooks, known as 'Subo' as some say he has a passing resemblance to Susan Boyle. Having met and interviewed Jack a couple of times, along with him giving up his free time to write the foreword for this book, I wouldn't be so rude as to insinuate such a thing. Lazar Marković of Liverpool, however ...

Brooks himself told me that a chap at Northamptonshire where he started his professional career had one of the better nicknames in the game. David Murphy was described as being like the Rain Man portrayed by Dustin Hoffman. However, because he wasn't quite as 'special', he was known as 'The Drizzle Man'.

Ian Bell meanwhile was known as 'The Shermanator' from *American Pie* due to his resemblance to the geek in the film. Others are just known by their initials such as Colin Cowdrey with MCC, or Mike Atherton who was known as FEC. This was supposedly a name given to him in his younger days when he was considered the 'Future England Captain', but after returning to Lancashire after his stint at Cambridge University it stood for something else, the middle word being 'Educated'. I will leave you to work out what the first and third words were, but needless to say we try not to use such profanities in such an upmarket volume as this.

At our club we pride ourselves on decent nicknames. One chap whose wife is called Eileen is known as 'Dexy's' after the band Dexy's Midnight Runners – I am sure you can remember what their biggest hit was – while another lad called Saqib (or Saq for short) is known as 'Scrotal'. I got the nickname 'Seve' after a particularly bad run of form with the bat while skippering the 1st XI back in the 1990s, a time when Mr Ballesteros was the 'non-playing captain' of the Ryder Cup team.

I am sure even reading this article you're thinking what name to give to your team mates. Every cricketer has to have one.

47
THE DAY VIV GOT A GOLDEN DUCK

Very, very occasionally your cricket club will host the professionals. I'm not talking about us as clubbies having a couple of decent seasons and getting snapped up. This is more about when county professionals have a benefit game at your club. There is a trend now, and also a decent moneyspinner, may I hasten to add, of having Lashings bring a side of professionals to you. The PCA do the same and for a mere £10,000 you can have a team of superstars visit. I'm not saying this happens at every club, but you might find yourself lucky enough to be in this position. If anyone offers you a game like this, please take it.

Here is a story from the 1970s, of when Viv Richards played a benefit game in Somerset, and got a first-baller against the might of Cheddar CC.

My uncle, a chap by the name of George Berry, was playing in this game and he recalls that Cheddar – far from the days of having the likes of Jos Buttler in their side – were a mixture of farmers, school teachers and the odd local solicitor. Somerset meanwhile, sent down a side including Botham, Richards, Denning, Dredge, Moseley, Kitchen and Close among others.

The day was a benefit game for Graham 'Budgie' Burgess and the locals had to guarantee him £750, which was quite a sizeable sum back in those days. It wouldn't get Beefy a replacement Saab, but it was still a decent amount of dosh. More or less the whole village turned out and a sizeable crowd waited to see the internationals smash it all over the place at the scenic Sharpham Road ground.

My uncle had a bowl early on at Dasher Denning and Ian Botham and they nurdled him around for a couple of twos, no doubt troubled by his away swing. After a while, Viv came in amid hushed excitement from the spectators. Remember this was a man who had taken England for a sparkling 291 a few years previously.

Cheddar had an off-spinner by the name of Ron Owen who was no doubt about to have his bowling figures seriously ruined. The first ball was just short of a length, and Viv made to hit it for a huge six. He stopped mid-shot – which as we all know is a fatal mistake – and the ball dollied up into the air straight back towards the safe hands of Ron. It was safely pouched, much to Ron's obvious delight!

As it was up in the air, the whole ground shouted for him to drop it, but as Ron said later, 'Do you think I could tell my grandchildren I deliberately dropped Viv Richards?'

A few years later Viv was being interviewed by the wonderful Brian Johnston during a lunch break and the subject of the Primary Club arose. The Primary Club is an organisation for all those who have suffered a golden duck at some point in their career. Johnners asked Viv if he would qualify as a member of such a fine establishment, and the great Antiguan replied that 'Yes, it was against some minor club or other.'

A few moments later someone phoned through recalling the above story and giving full details. Ron denies it was his handiwork! Viv no doubt, still remembers his visit to Cheddar back in the 1970s, but I bet not quite as fondly as Ron does.

48
WHEN THE PRO MEETS THE CLUBBIE

With the advent of Premier League cricket and the counties allowing their players to compete in some of the stronger leagues, club cricketers are more exposed to playing professionals than ever before. However, it has not always been the case, often resulting in devastating effects on the poor clubbie, and the psychological scars can sometimes take years to heal!

During a chat a few years ago with a mate of mine called Scott Ruskin over a quiet seven or eight Guinnesses, I was reminded of such a mismatch. Scott always refers to me as 'Dangerous Dan' as he always ends up with a horrendous hangover any time he goes anywhere near me, and this was one of those nights – although I just about remembered the story. Clubbies will often become good mates with other clubbies and you will build up a camaraderie with people from rival clubs. Anyway, Scott was explaining how he had the fortune to represent the Minor County Hertfordshire in the Cheltenham & Gloucester competition. This, if you remember, was the renamed NatWest or Gillette Cup (to those of a certain vintage) and Hertfordshire entertained Worcestershire in 2001.

Having removed the Worcester opener Willie Weston for 2, the bowler was feeling very pleased with himself until one of his team mates piped up with, 'You fucking idiot, now you've got Hick in earlier than we thought.' The man from Zimbabwe proceeded to help himself to a cheeky 155 as the Midlanders thrashed Herts by 267 runs! Hick also said after the game that Hertfordshire were mad to prepare such a road, as normally, whenever a Minor County entertains one of the big boys, a track about as even as Carlos Tevez's neck is prepared in an effort to even up the gap in class.

Another story of a similar nature comes via our mate Thorpster who played for a works team with a chap who played for Dover CC in the Kent League in the 1970s. Again, having picked up a couple of wickets in the first over and with the oppo on their knees at 0-2, the bowler was full of beans before the number four strode out to the wicket. One of the fielders then piped up with 'Fuck me, it's John Inverarity', as the Aussie Test player took guard. The Western Australian skipper, who was once bowled by Greg Chappell for a duck with a ball hitting a rather unfortunate sparrow in mid-air and taking a wicked deflection, proceeded to make the Dover bowling feel like that sparrow did, and soon ruined the openers' splendid figures as he smashed them all around the park on his way to a hundred and plenty.

Talking of Australians, it was during this era that my club managed to pick up Aussie Test player Ray Bright. Having toured England in 1977 and 1981, the left-arm spinner had married our first team skipper's sister and our local neighbours Southgate were none too pleased as they prepared to give us our annual thrashing. The supposedly strongest club in our area didn't see the funny side of being skittled for around a hundred, as the Victorian picked up 8-33. We didn't beat them too often it has to be said.

Fast forward 14 years and Southgate were again on the receiving end of a Test player from the southern hemisphere. A young and extremely rapid Chris Cairns had come to play for Cockfosters and basically bounced out the whole Southgate top order. At 7-5 they were struggling somewhat, and a few of us were watching in awe from the neighbouring pitch. Steve Rowe, the Southgate stalwart and opening bat, was unimpressed as he walked past us hissing, 'Well, we're not used to facing fucking Test match opening bowlers.'

I was also the victim of the gulf in class as a 15-year-old and playing for our under-17s in a league game versus Tottenham. Their opening bat had already hooked our pace bowler for six off the first ball of the game and second ball skied one towards me where both I and a team mate called at the same time, before leaving the catch to each other and watching disconsolately as the ball dropped between us. He went on to score a mere 120 not out, and within weeks had become the youngest century-maker for Gloucestershire at the age of 17. His name …? Mark Alleyne.

Mark Ramprakash regularly now plays for Stanmore in the Middlesex Premier League and Owais Shah plays for Welwyn

Garden City in the top division in Hertfordshire. With internationals such as Monty Panesar, Kevin O'Brien and William Porterfield, along with many recently retired county professional plying their trade in the top division of the Hertfordshire League, many clubbies are feeling the wrath of the player who is still good enough to show the gulf in class.

Cricketers these days are exposed to playing against the professionals more and more, and the likes of Gareth Berg at Middlesex and the foreword writer of this book, Jack Brooks, now at Yorkshire, are two who have arrived via the Home Counties Premier League. Saying that, Berg still gets teased by Rob Key of Kent that he is a 'clubbie'.

Those two players give hope to those of us who play for fun, as well as the aspiring youngsters coming through in club cricket. However, for those of us of a certain vintage, it's enough to induce nightmares.

49
THE GROUNDSMAN

As all of us get ready for a summer of cricket, there is one person hoping that the water level subsides and he can get his work done. As February turns into March, spring arrives and no one in cricket is busier than this bloke. As we huff and puff for an hour at winter nets, he's already out there in the middle. Red-faced, sweaty and most probably likes a drink, I bring you someone that every good cricket club needs. I bring you the groundsman.

The chances are your groundsman likes a drink. My first recollection of this was as a lad at North London CC watching the groundsman sit at the end of the bar putting it away, although it was much to my surprise as a 12-year-old to see him running out of the bar catching sick in his hands one evening. Never was someone with the surname List more appropriately named. For some reason unbeknown to man, as night follows day, as Arsenal go out in the knockout stages of the Champions League, this man who does your ground will love a beer.

You'll know who the groundsman is. Normally sporting a permatan, he is generally the one having a row with the opening bat who has been out for a duck that day. If you can't blame the umpire, the track is the next best thing. Some opening bats out there never leave a gate, play around a straight one or follow one to the slips, trust me.

The groundsman is no doubt a grumpy bastard, too. He treats his pitch with love and attention as if it were a new girlfriend, only for it to rain on a Saturday morning. That is when his beloved square gets ripped up by not only bowlers, or batsmen leaving a moon-sized crater while taking guard, but fielders too. This pisses groundsmen off no end, trust me – especially when he has 'advised' not to play on it only for a promotion-chasing or relegation-threatened skipper to go against his wisdom.

The groundsman, or curator as he is known in the southern hemisphere, can also do a passable impression of Michael Fish, too. Except that he generally gets it right. His knowledge of local weather is unsurpassed and some of the more forward-thinking groundsmen have state-of-the-art weather apps these days, too. Most, however, prefer the old-fashioned approach of wetting their finger and sticking it in the air.

The groundsman can be an impatient man, especially if the bar is open. If you have a number eleven that struggles to know which end of a bat to hold, the mower will be heard to start as he is on his way out to the middle. The groundsman is not a man to be messed with, especially at the Old Rec at St John's, where they used to get the guys from the prison next door to sort the pitch out. I reckon Brian Lara owes a few of those boys after his 375 and 400 there.

Yet these people should be loved and cherished – groundsmen that is, not the inmates of St John's nick. For them, the season is March to November. As soon as germination starts at 10°C, this man is in business cultivating his square. In September, when your kit is going into the loft, he deep drills or scarifies or gets the thatch out of the square. His work is not done when the cricket finishes.

During the season, he does the most boring job in the world and that is sitting on a roller going up and down. A cricket square needs a lot of rolling. Mowing, moving sightscreens and putting out ropes for you. Then you turn up at 12.15 on a Saturday expecting it all to be done. No wonder he can be a cantankerous old sod. They are also under pressure. Many an amateur skipper will lean on him if he has a good quick or spinner, or for that matter if the opposition have. Even at Test level the amount of five-day 'Chief Executive's' pitches we have seen in recent years are a testament to that.

They are the unsung heroes of cricket and despite their idiosyncrasies they are knowledgeable, decent folk who love the game. Every good cricket club needs a groundsman and if you have a good one, it makes a huge difference. When you turn up in April and your ground looks as manicured as Cheryl Cole, then you know why.

When the season starts, give your groundsman a hug. Better still, buy him a pint.

50
THE POST-MATCH PINT

The cacophony of laughter, the smell of beer and even the odd cigar is how I remember my childhood growing up in cricket clubs as the two sides who had fought out a hard game of cricket during the day now mingled freely in the summer dusk. But are these days a thing of the past? What has happened to the post-match pint? Where has one of the important social traditions in club cricket gone?

As a youngster playing in adult cricket at the age of 14 it was drummed into you that you stayed after the game. In those days sides would buy the other team two jugs – one lager and one bitter – and it would be down to the younger members of the side to go and take the jug around to the opposition. Needless to say that whatever was left ended up in our glass, bitter or lager, often both. It was ambidexterity at its best.

Older members of the side would often talk with other older members of the opposing team, people who they had played against for years. Those who had scored a fifty or had taken five wickets would also buy a jug which they took around the clubhouse. As a teenager it taught me social skills and it didn't matter who was in the opposition. The beauty of cricket back then was that you had builders and plumbers having a beer with doctors and judges. The barriers to social mobility were all broken down by our beautiful summer game.

I was taught that 'whatever happened on the pitch, stayed on the pitch' and many friendships were formed with people from other clubs. Problems were sorted out between the two teams in the days before clubs went running to the league disciplinary committee for every indiscretion in the law book.

It was as much a law in cricket that you stayed in the opposition bar for two or three pints, and they did at yours the following season. Valuable club funds were being taken over the bar as 11 players plus an umpire and a scorer would add to the financial coffers of other clubs, as they would to yours respectively. It was fiscal responsibility to keep the cricketing economy of clubs in the black, back in the uncertain economic times of the early 1990s.

So what has happened to those halcyon days? Some sides now don't even come and visit the opposition bar. Tea money and umpires' fees are exchanged within the confines of the dressing room. Even those who do stay often have a swift one for the road and are in their cars within half an hour of the last wicket falling or the winning run being hit.

Is it a by-product of the worsening behaviour in cricket these days? Quite possibly. Or then again, perhaps it is the reason.

Sides definitely do not socialise together as much these days. That they don't get to know each other over a period of years could be behind the worsening behavioural standards in the game. The younger members of the teams don't seem to know each other so well these days, often popping into the bar post-match for an energy drink, before they're off for their ice bath. There is a case that if these individuals had a beer with their opposition, there would be a marked improvement in the disciplinary standards in the game. Players would understand these people as human beings and not just someone 22 yards away whom abuse can be fired at on a Saturday afternoon.

Another reason is probably choice. This is definitely behind the slow strangulation of Sunday cricket in this country. People have more choice in life and the difference in lifestyle between 30 years ago and today is significant. Trading and licensing hours have definitely had an impact on the numbers of people playing club cricket on a

Sunday. Back then, faced with an episode of the *Thorn Birds* or *That's Life* on a Sunday night, most people I knew would choose their cricket club bar. Esther Rantzen came a distant second. Take a game of Sunday cricket in the current era and you will find that many cricket clubhouses are shut by 9.00pm. Those that are open have a handful of club diehards.

The clampdown on drink driving and the stiffer penalties rightly shown to those who break the law on this are also a reason.

Higher-standard Saturday cricket also takes its toll. All-day cricket makes life difficult enough for the family man, without him having four or five beers after play. Premier Leagues often mean travelling vast distances to the other end of a county. A combination of travelling time, warm-ups, all-day cricket and a wife with two young children and it's hard for this type of player to stay and indulge in a vital part of the fabric of the game.

It isn't just in club cricket either. In the current professional game, players are often on coaches and away from the ground quickly after the game. Back in the crazy scheduling of the 1970s and '80s you'd often get sides playing a John Player League game in the middle of a Schweppes County Championship match. The parties thrown by Ian Botham on the Saturday night of a Test were legendary – this in the days when players had the Sunday rest day. Certain players were out every night.

So it seems that the post-match pint and 'oppo speak' might be confined to the pages of cricketing history. Perhaps it belonged in the era of the Gray-Nicolls Scoop, the Duncan Fearnley Run Reaper, the St Peter mittens as endorsed by Tony Greig, or hedgehog gloves... It's a shame, as for me, it's an integral part of the game and teaches you great life skills.

Then again, we could always try to change the culture of our younger players.

51
THE STAYER AND THE SLAPPER

Umpiring a game of club cricket, one of our opening batsmen was grinding out a score on a difficult wicket and was soon joined by a dashing middle-order batsman who quickly outscored him. The opening bowler chirped up, 'Come on lads, let's think about this and get the field right here, we've got a stayer and a slapper. The story of my love life.'

52
THE SCORER

Towards the end of your cricket season you might finally notice someone who has followed the team around all year. This person will go to home and away games and yet you have never spoken to them. Who is this person who never speaks but carries a variety of multicoloured pens around with them? And then it suddenly dawns on you, it's your scorer.

Scorers come in all shapes, sizes, ages and genders. They range from the downright attractive female to the socially inept single man. They are a breed who prefer to spend their summers under cover, so the spring sees them having to disturb the local vagrant who has inhabited their score box as their winter abode.

Scorers are stat-obsessed. 99.99% of them also suffer from obsessive compulsive disorder. You mess with their scorebook and this meek, mild-mannered individual who doesn't say anything all year will suddenly combust. Neatness and order are the hallmarks of their work and they will go into huge bouts of depression should the coloured pen they've used for the opening bowler suddenly run out in his fourth over. Some have even been known to shout out to the skipper to take someone off rather than have to use two colours for the same bowler. They also go mental if it starts to rain and there's no cover for them. To see their book, so lovingly cared for, suddenly resemble an abstract finger painting that your 5-year-old would bring back from primary school fills them with angst. Then the skipper goes and leaves their book behind in the opposition clubhouse, leading to more despondency.

The more technologically advanced of this genus now carry laptops with them and go about their weekly task online. The advent of apps such as Total Cricket Scorer and websites like Play Cricket, mean that you can follow the fortunes of your club from miles away. Many scoreboards are now electronic and the score can show on the board from the safety of the pavilion, with batsmen's scores, overs and even runs required being sorted by a small contraption. The days of having to hook metal numbers on to a board and cutting yourself on the rusty nail that they dangle on are long gone. The scorers of yesteryear always had to have up-to-date tetanus jabs.

Long gone, too, are the rollers that required extreme precision to get the number just right so the players could actually decipher the score. These would hang half way between the numbers and gave a vigorous workout to all and sundry. You had to be fit to be a good scorer back in the day. Some clubs still have the drawstring ones that you have to pull down manually. Many a clubbie who has to go into the box with the opposition scorer (due to your club not providing one), will pull the string too hard leading to it coming off in his hand.

The other contraption is the scoreboard that you have to turn the dials clockwise or anti-clockwise to move the score. Often a standalone device, you still see this used when the electronic scoreboard technology breaks down or if the host club have failed to put 50p in the meter. These archaic boards have flummoxed many a club cricketer over the years and watching your lads trying to work out how to operate one of these is similar to watching a dyslexic read *War and Peace*. It's normally at this point that the 12-year-old opposition scorer steps in and sorts it out with a simple flick of the wrist.

The scorebox can be a strange and unpleasant place. You wouldn't venture into one for any reason other than to score a game of cricket. Aside from being a great habitat for tramps, they are littered with spiders, woodlice, earwigs and plagues of insects that you've only read about in the Old Testament. There are holes in the roof and in the floor, and a viewing hole at the front which is often strategically placed to funnel bitter northerly winds in April. Others involve climbing great heights too, often up precarious ladders and require crampons and the like to get you safely back down.

For those who operate at ground level, the players don't help them. Apart from losing a pen, nothing winds the scorer up more than a group of players standing in front of them so that they can't see the action. This usually means that they miss a run or a call of wide and get shouted at by the umpire for the lack of acknowledgement on his signal. Scorers don't like getting shouted at by umpires and it's usually by a player distracting them or standing in their line of vision that's the cause. The cry of 'Scorers' light' will be heard if they are polite, or 'You don't make a very good window, you know?' Then you have the batsman desperate to look at his runs in the book after a decent knock who again will stand directly in front of the sight line of the scorer. Many scorers give a more than passable impression of Bez out of the Happy Mondays as they weave from side to side trying to get a glimpse of the action with players in front of their beloved score box.

There are now courses that these people can go on. The ECB's Association of Cricket Officials run not only courses for umpires but for scorers too.

It's a tough job being a scorer. I believe that a tenner is the going rate these days, which is a vast improvement on the £1.50, a lemonade and a packet of crisps that I started on as a 12-year-old in club cricket. There can be serious pressure at times and woe betide them if they start to get the overs wrong in a tight finish. I knew of one child in the past who just gave up and went home half way through a game. It was only after 10 minutes when the board hadn't moved and the umpire was repeatedly shouting, 'Telegraph' from the middle that the players had realised what had happened.

The scorer's life has become easier though. They don't have to work out averages any more as this is all done online, should someone have had the inclination to upload the scorecard onto a cricket website. It has been known that when this is left to some players, those that get a duck or go for no wickets for 50 runs off of six overs can 'forget' to upload that scorecard. At the other extreme, the player who scores big runs or takes a five-wicket haul will upload this within 10 minutes of the game finishing.

Sometimes a scorer has to work alone due to the opposition not turning up with one. In this instance they will send a lower-order player into the scorebox when they are batting, but when they are fielding the solitary scorer has to manage everything alone. It can also lead to some hilarious mistakes. The cry of the question 'bowler's name?' will be heard at this point and trying to hear the mumble of a player in the wind from 70 yards away can often lead to the name being entered incorrectly into the book. I have had a team mate called Flatt entered into the book as Pratt in one of these instances and I dread to think what Northamptonshire's Ben Duckett was deciphered into during junior cricket.

The scorer is last to leave the field after a game, as they have to work out the bowling figures. They are also the last to tea as well. Look after your scorer, they save you a hell of a lot of hassle and should be treasured.

Just don't expect to have a good laugh over a beer with a good 99% of this stat-obsessed breed, though.

53
CRICKETING EXCUSES

Rarely is a batsman out to a decent delivery that was angled into middle and leg and moved away to hit the top of off stump. Rarely is a batsman out to a bowler that was too good for him. Even more rarely is a batsman out lbw working around a straight one that is going to hit middle stump about a third of the way up. Instead you will hear excuses as to why he was out.

Cricketers are a superstitious lot and this ranges from the direction in which you walk around your cricket club pitch to putting your right pad on first. However, judging by what I have heard, these are often cited as reasons why your team has just been rolled over for 50.

Watching team mates can also bring out the excuses. One of your lads might be batting beautifully and as he moves into the late 80s, the cry will go up 'no one must move'. Despite the fact that he takes half an hour in the nervous 90s and you are so desperate for a pee that the urine in your bladder is crystallising, if you get up and go and he is out, then it will be all your fault.

The sun can often play its part, too. I have heard batsmen moan about the sun reflecting off players' glasses to getting parked cars to move. One batsman at our club even suggested that we turned the square around as one end faced westwards. When it was pointed out to him that his dismissal of wiping one across the line to midwicket wouldn't make much difference, he argued his point vociferously. Fielders have used this on many an occasion after dropping game-changing dollies, despite it being their home ground and knowing the conditions.

Players turning up late for games will often blame traffic, apologising profusely through a haze of boozy fumes from the night before.

Other excuses can be slow-scoring batsmen at the other end, Neptune being in a juxtaposition with Saturn and if your kids run across the sightscreen during the fall of a wicket then it is your fault for having them in the first place.

Bowlers blame the slope, the lack of turn, their run-ups, the pace of the pitch, the bounce of the pitch, in fact anyone but themselves.

Usually the umpire is at fault. Batsmen have almost always got a bat on lbws or they have pitched outside of leg stump. If all else fails the umpire is the man to blame.

Either him or the groundsman.

54
SPIRIT OF CRICKET?

Umpiring a game on a hot day in 2016, one of the fielding side was shouting out "two" trying to get the batsmen to run a second, with the view to conning him and running him out. I informed him that this was against the Spirit of Cricket and had a word with his skipper. One of the batsmen who was on 120-odd at the time chimed in, 'Don't worry, but if he calls me for a three then I will tell him to piss off.'

55
THE DRESSING ROOM

A cricket dressing room is an extraordinary place. The site of a plethora of emotional outpourings, it can be either a sanctuary or a war zone, depending on the result. It can be a jovial place, with many jokes and stories of what the average clubbie got up to the night before. It can be a place where bad behaviour goes on among the lads that doesn't go on in the bar where there might be women and children present.

Before a game it can be a place where people get into the zone. Just before you step on the pitch it can be a place where the skipper rallies his troops and delivers his battle plans. I would advise club captains to do this once they have changed into their whites and not – as a club captain of mine once did – deliver this speech stark bollock naked. This can put some players off.

The openers will often pad up in silence, aided and abetted by the number three. If you are batting, you see a stream of lower order players visit the kitchen for a bacon and egg sarnie to soak up the previous night's excesses, to put a bet on or to get some sleep.

A cricket changing room can also stink like the camel enclosure at London Zoo. The aroma of sweat, stale beer, farts and old kit can make this a place that won't pass any hygiene standards. Dressing rooms with adjoining toilets can often be even worse as your opening bowler deposits the remnants of his Guinness.

After the game the dressing room, and not the adjoining toilet, can be a place where the skipper has a 'lock-in' after a poor performance. It is the place for finger-pointing and home truths.

Generally most players follow up with a shower. Club cricketers can often be juvenile in their outlook and various pranks and japes can go on in the shower. No matter how much shampoo is going into your eyes, you always need them wide open in this hive of merriment. Experienced clubbies will have had more shampoo soaked into their retinas than your average laboratory rabbit. It is not unknown for players to urinate on each other in the name of team bonding. Experienced aficionados can do this using no hands while shampooing their hair at the same time. Who said that men can't multi task?

Other shower-related jokes include pouring more shampoo on someone after they have just finished getting the first lot out of their flowing locks. Similarly some prefer to chuck shower gel over a team mate who has got out of the shower and spent five minutes drying himself off, meaning that he then has to revisit the taps.

Every club will have someone who forgets their towel. My co-author of the book *Cricket Banter*, Liam Kenna, once forgot his and having had an argument with our skipper for batting him too low in the order, picked up what he thought was our captain's off the peg, as he was showering. He took great delight in drying various parts of his anatomy in front of a few team mates, and had just hung it back on the peg, when a member of the opposition picked it up and walked off with it. Cue much hilarity from us.

There is also shower etiquette. When playing certain sides it is wise to let them use the showers first. No one wants to look like a 5-year-old boy who has just got out of a cold bath. Mark Ilott, the former England and Essex bowler, told me once that he was playing against the West Indians at Chelmsford and was between Junior Murray and Ottis Gibson. Brian Lara walked in, took one look at his anatomy and declared to him that 'he didn't have a cock, he had a clitoris'.

So dressing rooms are primarily the place for pranks. They are the place where the newspaper that you are reading can suddenly catch fire, or where a hot teaspoon that has just stirred your lunchtime cuppa can be pressed against an unwitting team mate's bare buttock.

Most of all they are a place where you will bond with your team mates.

56
JOCK ROT

Towards the end of the summer, especially if you are a wicketkeeper you will be afflicted by this dreadful disease. If you aren't a cricketer you will not have the faintest what I am talking about. Jock rot is the curse of all cricketers and leaves you in serious pain. It is the chafing of one's inner thigh and a sweat rash combined and makes every clubbie wonder if it is all worth it. Or more to the point, was the barmaid on tour worth it?

In April most of us clubbies invest in a new jockstrap. For the uninitiated this is an elasticated contraption that you step into with a pouch on the front that is for your box and cotton covering the elastic at the back, leaving one's buttocks bare on your whites. The person who invented such a thing obviously never faced a quick bowler. Either that or he had shares in Vanish or some other stain remover.

A new jock is a thing of beauty. Snugly fitting, it feels comfortable and early season goes unnoticed. It feels so nice, in fact, that you'd almost want to wear one out on a Friday night.

Come September, however it will make you walk into work like John Wayne when he steps off of his horse. The cotton has worn away towards the end of the season, leaving just the elastic bit inside to chafe. Nothing is as painful to the clubbie as a September century. It also loses its elasticity, leaving it to hang limply with bits hanging out of the sides like a disorientated octopus in an old fisherman's net. Think more testicles than tentacles, though.

Sometimes after a Saturday ton, they are even painful to actually get into on a Sunday. Not only that but they leave an awful red mark. What looks like a weal on the inner thigh from the middle of your leg to the crease of your buttocks, it is the curse of every club cricketer. It has been the reason for many a divorce in the UK and family lawyers will now ask the following questions to many a husband entering their office.

'Unreasonable behaviour?'
'No.'
'Adultery?'
'No.'
'Ah, jock rot…'

Despite the protestation of many a clubbie to the Mrs that you got it from playing cricket, she will simply not believe you. Wicketkeepers suffer most with all of the squatting down and getting back up again. Despite most glovemen suffering with knee- and finger-related problems due to the requirements of their trade, most will complain about jock rot above all else. Cricketers such as Vivian Richards or New Zealander Geoff Howarth are prone to piles for some reason or other, and jock rot is the precursor to an attack of the Plymouth Argyles.

It is the curse of the club cricketer, like drink was to the Victorian working classes – or, to quote Oscar Wilde, 'like work to the drinking classes'. It is the bane of your life and if you are lucky, it should finally heal by Christmas.

57
THE ANNUAL GENERAL MEETING

The final and most boring event in the calendar of the club cricketer's year is the Annual General Meeting. Generally held around November, this is the moment where revenge is taken on your skipper for batting you at eight all year when you deserved to be a five. This is the moment where two blokes who have been fairly harmonious team mates all season suddenly hate each other as they are both going for captaincy. It is not unknown for them both to be sent outside the room together as the voting starts, and they stand in frosty silence. The AGM can do some very strange things to people.

The AGM is something that you have to attend. If you don't then you can't moan about your skipper the following season. It is the time of year where all officers of the club are elected and every full subscription-paying member of a club has the right to vote, dependent on what is written into your club constitution. As cricket-loving ex-Prime Minister John Major once said, 'It's time to put up, or shut up.' You will find politicians having their own *Question Time* at every club.

Hosted in a freezing clubhouse, it's light years away from those summer months in the cricket season. You see that team mate who turns up in shorts all season long, with three layers of clothing and a duffel coat on. The clubhouse, which has had no one in it since the end of September and therefore no heating, feels like the interior of an igloo. This thaws after a while, but I'm not sure if this is because the heating has finally been turned up or because of all the hot air that is spoken at these events.

The AGM will start with a very boring speech by the club chairman. It is followed by even more boring rhetoric by the club treasurer. He will produce figures, spreadsheets, graphs and even Powerpoint slides and often paints a grim picture. Everyone looks intently at the profit and loss of the club, nodding their heads and pretending they understand any of it, only intermittently interrupted by some smart arse at the back of the room asking if we could save a few quid by using the tracing paper-style toilet rolls that haemorrhoid sufferers visibly blanch at the very thought of.

You then arrive at the exciting bit – if anything remotely to do with an Annual General Meeting can be described in such a fashion – the election of officers to the club. Firstly everyone needs to be proposed and seconded by the membership. It is at this point that people get railroaded into a job that they have no interest in doing, or more to the point that no one else within the structure of the club has any interest in doing. Long and stony silences are followed when the words 'Honorary team secretary, anyone?' are read out, quickly followed by thirty pairs of eyes looking to the floor, desperately trying not to catch the gaze of the club chairman.

Then you have the speeches by the proposer why this person would be good for the club. In every club across the land, no one will ever mention that this is because this person this person is their mate, family member, brother-in-law, business acquaintance, etc. This is another reason why large families dominate cricket clubs across the UK and beyond.

Then the voting starts. This is where things can become heated. I have attended AGMs where two individuals offered each other outside for a fight. It is not the best time for fostering team harmony. Other times you have individual members there who are not entitled to a vote. These people can take umbrage when told they can't participate in elections. Not paying an annual subscription can be one reason, not being a full member is another – perhaps instead they're only a social member or are family members who have been railroaded into coming so they can vote for their brother or husband for a captaincy role. Being told they can't vote, often goes down like a pork pie at a bar mitzvah.

Skilled and experienced politicians within the club use their wit and guile to outperform less erudite individuals at a club AGM. Other individuals use all of their charm and cunning to tell people to 'Fuck off'. One chap at our club many years ago used the clock. Fighting a losing battle, he knew that he had a hardcore of the support for his argument among the younger element of the club. His opponent had a few of the older element and he knew that the opposition support lived further away. Using his skill, he kept the argument going for as long as he could and as the clock ticked past midnight he could see that the other side's support was ebbing away, leaving one by one. He finally won the vote just before 1.00am as the opposition had finally succumbed to a combination of apathy, time constraints and general tiredness.

After the voting you get down to 'Any Other Business'. This is a minefield. A good chairman keeps this to a minimum – trust me on this one. This is where an AGM that is running smoothly can go through to the early hours.

AGMs can last an hour and a half if you are lucky. If you are unlucky they can be a good four hours. Starting at 7.45pm, they can go on late into the night, dependent on how harmonious the club as a whole is.

The AGM is many things, but is not a place for the faint-hearted. They are, however, a must for all clubbies to attend.

EPILOGUE

So, that more or less wraps up the clubbie's year, unless your club has a fireworks display to raise funds, helping cricket volunteers lose their fingers as they return back to that Catherine Wheel that didn't go off, or maybe your club has a Christmas do?

I am aware I have painted a bleak picture at times and although most of the stories here are true or based in some shape or form about cricketing people that I know from club level, it really isn't all that bad.

Cricket clubs are wonderful environments. They are safe places to bring your kids up in, they teach them good social skills and more importantly, they stop them from being glued to a screen all day. Cricket clubs get kids out in the fresh air and provided that you get sun cream and a hat on them, they are fantastic environments in which to grow up. Within every club is a wonderful cricket family at the heart of the community. They encourage monosyllabic teenage kids to mix and talk with people from different social spheres and again that can only be a good thing for their development.

Cricket clubs are struggling at present but everything is cyclical. Their day will come again and they will never die out. There are too many 'badgers' out there obsessed with the game, (me being one) for it to wither completely. As Jack mentioned in the foreword, they can be at the centre of the village during the summer months and despite the world moving forward in technological, social and economic terms, there is still something about the local club that takes us back to days when life was a little bit nicer and people much kinder to each other.

Thank you for your time reading *The Definitive Guide to Club Cricket*. I am sure if you have ever been a volunteer at any cricket club then some of the characters in the book will resonate with you. This one goes out to you.

Long live club cricket!

15635471R00097

Printed in Poland
by Amazon Fulfillment
Poland Sp. z o.o., Wrocław